Laundromat Millionaire

ADVANCE PRAISE

"Dave Menz is the real deal. He knows the laundromat business inside and out from hard-fought experience, intentional learning, and a vast network within the industry. His heart is one of a teacher and a giver, and there is no better person in this industry to learn from and to be guided. I highly recommend his book and consultation if you're in the market for a laundromat or want to optimize your laundromat business. *Laundromat Millionaire* is ten out of ten - only because the scale doesn't go higher!"

—**Jordan Berry,** Founder, Laundromat Resource

"I instantly knew that Dave was the real deal. Working with hundreds of laundromat owners in my career, it is a rarity to find one like Dave. He is passionate and enthusiastic about the impact he makes in the world by providing clean clothes to the communities he serves. It is a pleasure to publicly recommend his book and coaching, in which he displays his eagerness to help others succeed in a business that he, too, has found tremendous success. Talk about paying it forward."

—**Dennis Diaz,** Founder, SPYNR Digital Marketing

"I can directly point to Dave Menz's coaching as a $150,000 increase annually in my company's profits. His positive attitude and heart for service lead the way. I commend him for sharing his knowledge of all things 'laundry business' in *Laundromat Millionaire*. It will talk and walk you right through any challenges, and help you grow as a person and in business."

—**Ken Wales,** Founder, Happy Laundry

"Every business owner should read *Laundromat Millionaire*. Overcoming trauma, obstacles, giving birth to family, businesses and hope, dreams coming true. Staying the course - no matter what. Dave is a master."

—**J Scott,** Investor, Adviser & Author

"*Laundromat Millionaire* exemplifies what is possible through smart work, determination and teamwork. If you are—or want to be—a business owner, this is a guidebook. Read it. And add it to your library for future reference/ inspiration."

—**Steve Millman,** H-M Laundry Equipment Company, Cincinnati, Ohio

"Dave's book is a demonstration of how you can build positive possibilities, business ethics, relationship elevation, and productive teamwork on a foundation of solid values and succeed as a business owner. This is one of those books you'll read again and again. Do yourself a favor and buy it today."

—**Dr. Joey Faucette,** GetPositive.Today

"*Laundromat Millionaire* exemplifies what is possible with smart work and determination. It entices the 'every man or woman', to reah high and never give up."

—**Curtis May,** Host of the Practical Wealth Show Podcast

Laundromat MILLIONAIRE

THE GRIT TO ELEVATE AN INDUSTRY

DAVE MENZ

NEW YORK

LONDON • NASHVILLE • MELBOURNE • VANCOUVER

Laundromat Millionaire

The Grit to Elevate an Industry

Published in New York, New York, by Morgan James Publishing. Morgan James is a trademark of Morgan James, LLC. www.MorganJamesPublishing.com

Proudly distributed by Ingram Publisher Services.

A FREE ebook edition is available for you or a friend with the purchase of this print book.

CLEARLY SIGN YOUR NAME ABOVE

Instructions to claim your free ebook edition:
1. Visit MorganJamesBOGO.com
2. Sign your name CLEARLY in the space above
3. Complete the form and submit a photo of this entire page
4. You or your friend can download the ebook to your preferred device

ISBN 9781631957864 paperback
ISBN 9781631957888 case laminate
ISBN 9781631957871 ebook
Library of Congress Control Number: 2021947664

Cover Design by:
Rachel Lopez
www.r2cdesign.com

Interior Design by:
Christopher Kirk
www.GFSstudio.com

Morgan James is a proud partner of Habitat for Humanity Peninsula and Greater Williamsburg. Partners in building since 2006.

Get involved today! Visit MorganJamesPublishing.com/giving-back

*"Growing up very poor, in a fairly rough environment,
you either have grit, you develop grit, or you don't make it."*
—Dave Menz, The Laundromat Millionaire

Grit, what does it mean? Millionaire, does it have meaning? Dave Menz, a working-class guy from Flint, MI, grew up in poverty and overcame superhero-like obstacles. This story is a life and business journey that doesn't stop at rags to riches. It *begins* with a stubborn and obsessive mission to be a business owner with a tenacious and genuine purpose to help others to do the same—even if you *also* do not have a college degree or perhaps *because* you have one.

If you think there is nothing sexy about a laundromat, think again. Dave says he had to give that measured deliberation, but what it boils down to is—if he can—*you* can.

In essence, how'd Dave become a Millionaire?
Well, nothing fell in his lap. He pursued it.
By scratchin', scrapin' and hustlin'—and foremost, his mantra:

Never Give Up.

Adversity can be a tough, but a good teacher, assuming you don't give up and quit. When opportunity knocks, open the dang door. Don't own a job, own a business—and leverage your time.

Laundromat and **Millionaire** are two words not often combined. If you follow the principles in this book, including: embody a thirst for knowledge, keep your hand out of the cookie jar, embrace the spirit of new revenue streams, put yourself in the way of mentors, cultivate a forward thinking vision, and sanction the savvy it takes to take risks…welcome.

If you have that kind of grit, you are on the path. This business can be a gold mine for a person who's full of grit and doesn't care about sexy.

If we are going to elevate our industry, we better get used to the term, **Laundromat Millionaire**.

The stories and examples in this book may focus on laundry…and, for a guy who has earned success in it, pay homage of course! It is a vital community resource that simplifies a life, and can improve a neighborhood. Yet, the many tenets pertain to perhaps all industries, and certainly the way we choose to do business. Read on….and you will bear witness to what works.

Everyone has unique gifts and talents. Success for most people is simply a matter of will. How bad do you really want it?

Do Not—Do Not—Underestimate True Grit

For my siblings Lisa & Danny, and to my baby boy Caiden.
All of you were taken from this earth way too soon and while I don't
understand why, your memory and love for others burns in me daily.
I vow to live my life as if every day is cherished. Because it is.
I miss you all so much and cannot wait to see you again someday.

CONTENTS

PREFACE

My mission is to elevate an industry, specifically the Laundromat Industry. I didn't exactly start with that objective in mind. I just wanted to be a business owner.

Here is a brief progression:

I thrived through family hardship, and learned the essence and value of grit.

I reveled in many insomniac-ish nights studying and learning from the greats in business.

And, I became a business owner of a laundromat after discovering it on Craigslist.

And then, the owner of a chain of businesses, Queen City Laundry.

And, I continuously practiced disciplined reinvesting of earned money.

And, I was rewarded with a phenomenal team.

And then, flourished in even more obsessive reading, and researching, and networking.

And, subsequent to that, I became the owner of real estate.

And, I prospered with a heckuva a lot of faith in God and myself.

Okay, enough ANDs, I'm out of breath.
Well, the books don't typically lie—accounting or otherwise—
Yup, I'm a millionaire.

As you know and will read, laundry just isn't sexy. Not on the surface. But as a business venture it certainly is. It's a vital community resource. It fills a fundamental need—whether your machine broke down at home or you do not have one there in the first place. And, when operated in a modernized and elite service manner, the local laundromat can be a welcome neighbor in the neighborhood—for economic reasons, and for convenience too.

I know my mission is to elevate an industry. It is also a vision to elevate lives. If a working guy like me can do it, so can you. Maybe you will read this story and be inspired. Maybe you will change the way you perceive that laundromat structure in your town or city, and maybe, just maybe you will be encouraged to follow what might be considered a path less traveled, but a path that sets you on a course to enjoying your day, your family, and personal freedom. The dollars count in personal freedom, but the feeling counts more.

Read on. Let me know what you think when you are done…or ready.

Own the grit within. Never give up,

Dave Menz
The Laundromat Millionaire

SECTION 1

WHAT ABOUT US?

Chapter 1

FAMILY ROOTS—THE RELEVANCE

*"Growing up very poor, in a fairly rough environment,
you either have grit, you develop grit, or you don't make it."*
—Dave Menz, The Laundromat Millionaire

A BIT OF BACKSTORY

On my mom's side of the family, my Grandma and Grandpa Whitley grew up very poor in the literal sense. They were raised in rural Arkansas during the Great Depression and their families literally picked cotton for a living. After a stint in the Navy and starting a family they moved from Arkansas to Flint, Michigan in search of a factory job at General Motors.

In the 1950's, American automobile manufacturing was helping to shape America into an economic superpower. At that time, it was well known throughout America that the automobile factories were hiring nearly all able-bodied men on the spot for jobs that had great pay and benefits. By the 1960's, one-sixth of all working Americans were employed directly or indirectly by the automobile industry, my family, on both sides, were no exception.

On the other side of my family, my Grandma Menz was born in Flint, and my Grandpa Menz's family moved there when he was around 11 years old. Both had grown up very poor during the Great Depression.

Married at a very young age, my Grandpa Menz dropped out of high school, lied about his age on his application (he was only 17), and began working in the GM factory to support his family. After being drafted into the Army and serving during the Korean War, he eventually returned to his job at GM.

My parents, Mark and Marlene Menz, met during the late 1960's and became high school sweethearts during the early 1970's. Although they lived in different parts of the Flint area, they met and spent a lot of time together in the Bristol Road Church of Christ youth group.

My brother, Danny, was born to 17 year old newlyweds in October, 1973. Danny had been conceived before my parents were married, but by the time he was born, they had married and were living in my Grandma and Grandpa Menz's basement trying to figure out what they were going to do next. After getting married, they realized that they needed a plan. Dad still had another year of high school in order to graduate.

Luckily, my dad was a pretty good student and only needed one credit in Civics in order to receive his diploma. Given the circumstances, the school worked it out so that he could take the class the first hour of the day, and then be dismissed. From there he would go to his full-time job at the local supermarket.

To this day, I can't imagine how scared Mom and Dad were to be married with a newborn at such a young age, but they trusted each other and trusted that God would show them the way. After my dad graduated from high school, he left the supermarket and obtained a full-time job at the school board office doing entry level work. I am sure he may have asked if this was his future. Therein, comes the advice of Grandpa Menz.

My Grandpa Menz was always the loving and protective type. One day he decided to have a talk with his son about his future. He told him that the GM factory was still hiring, and he could likely get him on if he wanted. My dad pondered the opportunity to immediately make good money and have full benefits for his young family.

However, knowing that Grandpa had been miserable working in the factories for his entire life, he decided that he wanted something more for his career. While he greatly respected those that worked hard in the factories, he knew it wasn't for him. He wanted more than just a paycheck and benefits, but he didn't know what.

Shortly after this conversation, my dad took the Air Force admissions test and scored very high. The recruiter was impressed. He told Dad that he could likely enter into the Air Force, go through basic training, and then enter a high skill area where he would get valuable training. This training could no doubt set him up for a career path outside the military.

My dad liked the sound of this a lot better than his other options, so off to boot camp he went. After boot camp my dad chose his career path, went through his training program, and was eventually stationed at the National Security Agency (NSA) in Fort Meade, Maryland. My parents lived there for the next few years and in May of 1976, had another baby boy that they named David. (That's me!) I was named after King David in the Bible.

THE RELEVANCE?

Why do I tell you these things about my background? Well, as I've aged and matured, I've learned that, like a foundation to a house, if we are going to learn from and inspire each other to achieve success, then we must start with the foundation.

The foundation of everyone's life is their backstory, and often their extended families' backstory. So, this is mine. While genetics certainly play a small part in who we become later in life, the reality is, our backstory and life story play a much more important role.

WHILE GENETICS CERTAINLY PLAY A SMALL PART IN WHO WE BECOME LATER IN LIFE, THE REALITY IS, OUR BACKSTORY AND LIFE STORY PLAY A MUCH MORE IMPORTANT ROLE.

As mentioned, during my young childhood, we were very poor. My parents were trying to live on entry level military pay with a family of three, and then eventually four. It was tough, very tough. We lived in military housing on base, and would often run out of money before the next paycheck. The fact that we were a long way from Michigan and didn't have any nearby family or friends in Maryland didn't make it any easier.

I suspect this is part of what bonded my parents together for life. It's amazing what adversity with nowhere else to run can do for bonding a young couple together. They married as teenagers and literally grew up and figured out life together - side by side, in a seemingly far-away place.

VALUE IN ADVERSITY

Adversity can be a tough, but a good teacher assuming you don't give up and quit.

One thing about my parents, neither of them have the word quit in their vocabularies. I guess that's likely where I get it from too. To this day, if you want to see me accomplish something, just go ahead and tell me that I can't do it. That's all of the motivation that I need, and I will not quit until I've proven you wrong. Equally important is the grit that was instilled in me at a young age. Growing up poor, in a fairly rough environment, you either have grit, you develop grit, or you don't make it.

Over the next few years, my dad saved up his military leave and went back home to visit family near the end of his enlistment. It was then that his old boss from the school district called, and offered him a better job working with computers at nearly double his military pay. While double of very little is still quite small, it was a move that he knew he had to make for his family. With this, Dad returned to civilian life and back to Flint, Michigan we moved.

The next few years of our childhood was spent in Flint, a blue-collar suburb outside of Detroit. But, that was home to us, and really all we knew.

After moving back home, my parents continued to struggle financially. After exiting the military, they quickly realized that they weren't much better off financially as civilians than they were in active duty with many of the perks received by military families. Every family I knew struggled. The ones with jobs at the GM shop (factories) did better than most, but no one was exactly thriving.

Despite the factories being seen as the best career opportunity in my hometown, like my dad, I aspired for something different, even from an early age. Although I don't remember this, Dad has told me the story of how at kindergarten graduation, they would ask all the kids what they wanted to be when they grew up. Apparently, while other kids answered with "*I want to be Batman*" or "*A professional baseball player,*" I answered that I wanted to own my own business.

All the adults in the audience likely laughed at how cute I was. Most people that we knew from Flint saw being an employee of someone else's business was the only option. Owning and building businesses was really no more removed than being Superman or a professional baseball player to them. In their minds, these were all naive pipe dreams, but we'd likely all end up either working at GM or in trouble with the law.

It's unfortunate, but oftentimes in poor environments, the well-meaning adults tamper with and even kill the dreams of young people by telling them to be "reasonable" or "practical." In their minds, working at GM was the ceiling for our lives. If anyone in your family worked at GM, you "had money". If not, you were likely poor, and we were poor, even if our grandparents were middle class…which was a bit of a big deal in the 'olden days'.

A QUICK STORY

During my childhood, our family experienced a fair amount of adversity, mostly financial, but the environment wasn't great either. As kids, we had what we needed for the most part, even if it meant that our extended family was helping to make ends meet. We drove unreliable and downright embarrassing cars, but then again, so did most people we knew.

I recall our unreliable family car breaking down in the middle of a snowstorm and us having no money for a tow or the repairs. We were parked on the side of the road, and I huddled with my brother and sister as the temperature dropped. I clearly remember the frustration and helplessness my parents felt.

My dad, being a proud man, would never really ask for help from anyone except his parents. Fortunately, my grandpa and grandma Menz were always there for us, over and over again.

Having grown up that way and knowing what I know now about my younger days, I understand how easily and quickly we could've been homeless or destitute if not for our extended families having good jobs at the factory. Most weeks, they didn't have a lot of extra in their budget. Yet, they were always there to help.

PEDAL OR PEDDLE

Though I didn't realize it at the time, I think these memories had a huge impact on me. Like my father, I am a proud man and never want to feel as they did when on the side of the road with their children. It also taught me the value of family - whether by blood or not - and the importance of being there for each other in times of need with zero expectation of reciprocity. I learned the value and relevance of the right thing to do.

One definite benefit of being raised poor was it taught us early on to work for anything we wanted. Like all kids, we loved riding our bikes down to the corner store for some candy. We knew Mom and Dad wouldn't have any extra money for our silly Boston Baked Beans, Lemonheads or anything chocolate, so we figured out quickly how to make the needed change for ourselves. We would ride for hours on many neighborhood streets, looking for just one more can, one more bottle. And, if we were lucky, we'd hit the motherload. Our legs ached and we worked up a sweat. But the search and effort were worth it. That "valuable" trash was needed to fund our sugar cravings. There was a reward ahead.

Lucky for us, in Michigan they have a bottle and can deposit of ten cents each. Basically, how this works is that when you purchase any drink in a can or bottle, you pay an extra 10 cents per item in a deposit. You get it back when you return the empties to the store.

IF YOU'VE NEVER HEARD THIS BEFORE, LET ME BE THE FIRST TO TELL YOU THAT WHILE BEING A CAPED CRUSADER MAY NOT BE IN THE CARDS, THE TRUTH IS THAT YOU CAN BE AND ACCOMPLISH ALMOST ANYTHING THAT YOU SET YOUR MIND TO.

Would I be as stubborn and as driven as I am today had I not been raised as I was?

Who knows, but undeniably it shaped me into who I am today. It may sound far-fetched to most kids today, but that was life as we knew it. If we wanted anything extra, we went on the hunt for those bottles and cans, even if we were only 7 years old. In that environment you learn it young, or you do without. I probably did some of both. Regardless, I refused to see a ceiling for myself, and I still carry that mindset with me everywhere that I go.

I refused to believe the garbage about not having options in life, no matter how many times I heard it. I made money out of what would be perceived as garbage after all! If you've never heard this before, let me be the first to tell you that while being a Caped Crusader may not be in the cards, the truth is that you can be and accomplish almost anything that you set your mind to. Find your sources of motivation. Ignore the noise. Go make it happen!

Even if you have to pedal, or peddle, first.

OWN THE GRIT WITHIN:

- *Stay focused. Your start does NOT determine how you will finish.*
- *Embrace adversity even though it can be tough. It is a good teacher assuming you don't give up and quit.*
- *Refuse to believe any garbage about not having options. You have them…or you make them.*

Chapter 2

FORGING FORWARD WITH FORTITUDE - ADDICTION, CANCER, DIVORCE & BANKRUPTCY

"Fortitude is the marshal of thought, the armor of will, and the fort of reason."
—Francis Bacon

The good news is that other than being poor, my life was a pretty stereotypical childhood. That is, until we moved to Cincinnati. While living in Cincinnati my parents became foster parents, and we resided at a home for troubled kids. Mom and Dad had big hearts, saw a need, and believed that God drew them to that place.

We moved onto the campus and within a few weeks my brother Danny, age 13, me at age 10, and our 5 year old baby sister, Lisa, had anywhere from four to six troubled girls living at the home with us. All had come from terrible backgrounds. Their stories would make a grown man cry. Surprisingly, some were fairly well adjusted, but of course some had very serious issues and we saw it all nearly every day.

FORGING THROUGH TURMOIL

BIG BROTHER DANNY

Unfortunately, during our time there, Danny was molested repeatedly by an almost 18 year old "girl" who'd had a very brutal history. She had been exposed to more in her life than anyone should ever see. My brother had always been my best friend until this point. This tragedy changed his life forever. After the abuse, he was never the same.

He eventually got into severe drugs, constantly ran away, and was just a lost, lost soul. While this didn't happen to me personally, we shared a bedroom and I lived through it right alongside him. I wasn't aware of the molestations at the time, but I was certainly knee deep in the aftermath, and it was brutal. In fact, it pretty much tore our family apart.

Once my parents became aware, we quickly left the children's home and moved to Amelia, Ohio, a suburb of Cincinnati. The house my parents found was modest, but it was ours and we were away from the chaos of the children's home. A relief for me, and I'm sure, for everyone.

Unfortunately, the damage was done, and our family would never be the same, especially my idol and big brother. Feeling blamed, wrestling with guilt, and turning to drugs to avoid it all, he struggled to cope with daily life. Even though we'd left the environment of the home, Danny's issues were set in stone, and they came with us to Amelia. While never meaning to, he wreaked havoc on our family in unimaginable ways and we never really returned to a peaceful manner of living.

Danny eventually became of age to move out, struggling with depression, anxiety, trust issues, low self-esteem and severe drug addiction for the rest of his life. Most people don't really understand the psychological damage abuse does to a person, let alone an entire family. Unfortunately,

I know all too well.

BABY SISTER LISA

As if struggling through Danny's teen years wasn't enough, my baby sister Lisa, at age 9, was diagnosed with a malignant (cancer) brain tumor. She, and our entire family, fought hard for years in hopes of remission for her.

We amassed the financial, spiritual, emotional stress of many Emergency Room runs, and several 8-9 hour surgeries by world renowned brain surgeons. Essentially, more than any prior hardship, it was hell on earth for our family.

Lisa fought hard for 5 years, but in 1995, I sat in Children's Hospital in Cincinnati and watched my baby sister take her last breath. She was only 14. I was 19. Too little life lived, and too much at the same time.

I could honestly write an entire book on the tragedy that our family endured, though that isn't what you're here for. Between watching my baby sister struggle and suffer, and living with my big brother as he worked through trauma and struggled with addiction, it was more than any family—any human being - should endure.

Yet there is more…

Danny eventually overdosed on heroin at the age of 39. Having lived with me several times throughout his tragic adult life, in 2013 he moved in with my family one final time. We thought he was doing well, participating in an outpatient rehab program, and a local support group. However, one afternoon, we found him cold, pale, stiff and lifeless on the floor of our basement.

The best friend and brother I had known, was forever gone.

FORTITUDE

While these events tore my family apart in every way humanly possible, I'm still amazed that my parent's marriage survived and remained intact.

The collateral damage to us all was immeasurable, but they remained loyal to each other and as in love as ever through it all.

While I don't want to bore you with the remainder of my upbringing, suffice it to say that my childhood was marred with a lot of painful tragedy, abuse, and a lot of adversity. All impacted me as a timid and weak child. Over time, it also transformed me into a very confident, strong and tenacious young adult. In fact to this day, there are many people in the world that think they know me and who I am, but if they haven't spent significant time with me since my mid-twenties, then they really have no idea.

I constantly reflect about how these tragedies can break some people to their core and others they just make stronger. I guess it's really true what they say, *"What doesn't kill us makes us stronger."*

While the backstory of my childhood in poverty and tragedies during my upbringing is important to understand, let's get down to business. How did I go from a poor kid to a successful, millionaire entrepreneur? Not immediately, for sure. The journey continues.

When I reached the age of 18, my parents were now firmly in the middle class. Dad had worked super hard over his career, been promoted many times, and was now earning a decent middle-class salary and benefits. They helped me a little with the costs of community college, but weren't really able to help much, and I knew it. If I wanted to get a college degree, it would really fall on my shoulders.

I enrolled at a local community college in Cincinnati, where I'd now lived since middle school. I was already living on my own, had a full-time job as an assistant manager at a local tire store, and my own apartment with some roommates. AND, I attended college full time. I was busy and stressed out, but I was independent, and no one could tell me what to do. Well, except my boss, and my professors, and my landlord. Ha ha!

During this crazy year of my life, I actually accomplished a lot for an 18 year old. I worked over 40 hours most weeks, took around 15 credit hours with a GPA in the high 3's, and acted as the responsible one in our apartment. Meaning, I collected the money, made sure the bills got paid, communicated with the landlord, arranged for repairs, and more.

However, after a year of this life I was just exhausted, and I had pushed myself to the limit with very little sleep. I found myself always being tired, irritable, and even sick way more than normal. I recognized this and knew something had to change, so I stopped going to college.

Like my dad years before me, I didn't know what I'd do at this education juncture. I did know that I had bills to pay now, and that college just wasn't in the cards for me.

Passion for Learning… What I Want to Learn

For my entire life, I'd been an underdog. I wasn't good at formal education which primarily required memorization. With a terrible memory, I'd always struggled. I'd had people mock and make fun of me for most of my life for "not being smart," though I always knew better. I always knew that I could do anything that I set my mind to, but if it wasn't important to me, then I'd likely underperform.

Yada…yada… I was constantly bullied for being poor and always having goofy, hand me down clothes. I was bullied for being overweight. I was bullied by other adults and teachers for my subpar grades, and constantly reminded of all of the reasons that I wouldn't be successful.

Let's now just call that what it is…Bullcrap! I am a freaking millionaire, and completely in love with what I do for a living. If that doesn't make me successful, then I don't know what does. That does not make me arrogant. It positions me to share what I learned, what I know…in the service of others.

Regardless of not being noted a scholar academically, ironically, I was always very naturally inquisitive. From a young age, I had a thirst for true information and knowledge, but I saw formal education as mostly a waste of time. I had to see the value in what was being taught and when I did, I became passionate about learning.

By this time in my life, I'd embraced the real world and realized I had a ton to learn, and little of it that I felt I needed or must know right now, was taught in school. I'd begun to develop an insane thirst for knowledge, mostly through books. I couldn't get enough.

In the hundreds of books that I read, I saw a common theme. The world is *full* of highly successful, gifted and motivated people, who for different reasons never obtain a college degree. Being fairly pragmatic in nature, I hard-headedly thought, well if they can do it, why can't I? Or possibly even more pragmatic, and realistic—*so* will I.

I realized that this "rule" in society, that you must have a college degree to be successful, is complete garbage. (Imagine that! Here we go with garbage again…) I knew that not all people with college degrees, and even graduate level degrees, are "smart" nor are they "successful". Note: I use quotes around "smart and successful", because in my mind's eye, and the minds of many, these terms are relative. In fact, I'd learned that for many people a degree is a crutch. Oftentimes, once they achieve their degree, they believe that they are entitled to success. WOW! What a disadvantage that is in life!

The advantage is realizing…that education, with degree or not, is a beginning. Thinking and forging ahead with fortitude? It is what you do with what you *choose* to learn that matters.

A QUICK STORY

I like to constantly refer to what I call the "Tom Brady Rule". Tom Brady is an American football player. Tom has never been known as the greatest pure athlete in the world, but he's always loved football. Early in life, he realized that if he wanted to compete with much bigger, stronger, and better athletes, he'd be forced to outwork them. He realized that it was the *only* way to even the playing field and give him a chance to play the game that he loved.

He enforced his work ethic in high school football, college football, and again in the NFL as a 6th round draft pick of the New

England Patriots. If you aren't aware, as of the writing of this book, Tom Brady was rounding out his football career. He has had a longer, and more accomplished career than anyone in NFL history. He is a veritably guaranteed first ballot Hall of Fame Player, and arguably *is* the best quarterback, and even player, to ever play in the NFL.

If in doubt, give Tom Brady a quick Google search, and you will read about a family who overcame adversity—and evidently—no, obviously—this mindset and skill set of never give up was instilled in Tom Brady.

Why is this brief Brady homage important to education? Or, perhaps as pertinent—why is it critical for you to think about it as it pertains to the development of your skills and raw or latent talent as you pursue your passion(s)? Read on.

EXERCISE YOUR WILL

The fact is, if we truly want to be successful, we will find a way. Now to be fair, I'm not a hater of a university education. It can be a critical tool to have in your tool belt for specialists like doctors or lawyers. Certainly, a necessity. Yet, I know many incredibly "smart and successful" people with, and without, a college or university degree. The fact is, if we want to be successful, we will find a way.

Everyone has unique gifts and talents and success for most people is simply a matter of will. How bad do you really want it?

Let me reiterate before the critics storm on me. I'm not here to tell you that having a college degree is a bad thing. It's a credential that is better to have than not. And, the socialization can be a positive education too. What I am telling you is that I've seen a tremendous number of people buy into the societal belief that because they have a degree, they are somehow owed success, and it ends up being their downfall.

If it so happens that the diploma on your wall stops you in your personal progress - reconsider. And, I strongly suggest you consider…is it serving you as a crutch or a leg up? Are you limping along or springing forward?

I want NO ONE to be stopped because they don't have a degree. I want everyone to see his or her possibilities in any vocation or as an entrepreneur and business owner. Do not let doubt get in the way. There are millions of success stories regarding those that did not have a college education, but made their way very successfully. If that path is for you—stay on it!!

Suffice to say, create your possibilities with your natural inquisitiveness and elbow grease that is engaged by your interests and passions. Define your desired outcomes, and your own definition of smart and successful—that is the definition which you can manifest and *own*.

SPEED BUMPS

Be the Tom Brady in your field of interest and garnered expertise, and it's very likely that good things will follow—but only, if you get out of your own way. The bumps in the road, real or perceived, are also part of your education.

Forward another few years of life and living…

When I was 19, a family friend told me about an entry level job opening at the local telephone company, Cincinnati Bell. It was actually a significant pay decrease from where I was working. However, she described for me how Cincinnati Bell offered in-house training, and almost always promoted from within. I was sold! While the pay was terrible to start and the hours even worse, I knew this was my opportunity to a better life.

I also knew that I'd have to crawl through the sand if I ever wanted to get to the ocean.

I rolled up my sleeves, excelled in this entry level position, worked my tail off and was eventually promoted. I was promoted just in time for my daughter, named Tannah, to be born. And now, my girlfriend and I could get our own apartment, take care of our baby, and get married.

Within a couple years, we were divorced.

Having no real financial education, she and I had over-leveraged our personal finances. The divorce was financially devastating. I was forced to file bankruptcy. I'd had many lows in my life, but this was a new one for me. Despite my best efforts, I was a divorced, bankrupt, uneducated, single Dad.

At age 25, I was a complete failure in my mind. I'd failed at marriage. I'd failed to keep my family together, making me see myself as a failure as a dad. I'd failed at getting a college degree. And, I'd even failed at basic personal finance.

From the outside, I looked like a successful middle-class man, but it all came crumbling down in a matter of minutes and it hurt, really, really bad! In the process, I didn't realize I was doing it, but I'd built a house of cards.

Little did I know at the time, that nearly every successful person has experienced a similar time in life. I didn't realize that the overwhelming data shows that people who rarely take chances or fail at anything in their lives, also rarely accomplish much. They just kind of get by.

For a second, I believed the voices of my past. I believed that all of those people were right and that I was indeed a failure. I almost started to believe my own voice in my head. That's when my natural tenacity, stubbornness and curiosity brought me back to earth. I started reading and researching why, and how, people fail. I knew in my stubborn bones I could learn from my failures, and that I'd be wiser and more prepared for success.

This is the middle class as we know it in America, honest, hard-working people in almost every case, but also people who are usually paralyzed by fear and afraid to ever take a chance on ourselves. This is oftentimes the reason that we never achieve what we are fully capable of. I was determined to not get sucked into that cycle of mediocrity, even if it meant falling down a few times in the process.

I suppose the benefit of growing up with nothing is that I didn't really have anything to lose. I researched for hundreds of hours how to be a good dad, a good husband, and a successful adult. While I didn't know how or what or even where, I knew that I would someday be successful.

What gave me this confidence you ask?
I refused to quit until I was successful. I knew that I'd been knocked down several times in this fight that we call life, but that the fight wasn't over. You never know who will make an impression on your life, and I've had many people do so. One was someone I barely knew, but I remember her insightful reminder that I may be young, but I now had all this valuable life experience! I knew this was right! At this singular moment, I bounced back mentally, quit feeling sorry for myself, and I was now more confident than ever.

If I'm honest, most people didn't really understand my newfound confidence either. I guess because they'd likely never experienced failure. They viewed my failures as a permanent thing, while I viewed them as not only temporary, but also an important part of the learning process on my way to success.

While I was disappointed and let down, I now saw myself with two choices. One, I could get back up, *learn* from my failures and mistakes, and allow that education to make me stronger. Or, two, I could simply crumble, shrink and settle for the life in front of me. So, I did what I'd always done before. I got back up and dusted myself off.

While we don't always have a choice over what happens to us, we do have a choice of how we react to those things. I'm not a failure because I've failed. I'm a success because I've failed. I used those experiences to make me a better version of myself. In fact, I've adopted this mentality and apply it every single day of my life.

In life, we ALL experience adversity. No one is immune. What separates us is what we do with it. Some of us allow tragedy, pain, and failure to define us or paralyze us with fear. Others decide it is exactly what they needed to catapult themselves to becoming the person that they really want to be.

OWN THE GRIT WITHIN:

- *Develop a thirst for knowledge. Read, listen, dream, sleep, find those superheroes who you will learn from.*
- *Always view failure as temporary. View it as a learning experience. Failure is NOT permanent, and it does NOT define us!*
- *Choose your way forward. How will you react or respond?*

Chapter 3

SCRATCHIN', SCRAPIN' & HUSTLIN'

"The dream is free. The hustle is sold separately."
—Unknown

With a newfound confidence in myself, I was starting to figure out who I was. My love for business and entrepreneurship was never far from my mind and this confidence helped tremendously. Business, the idea of it and finding ways to make money, were always a focus.

When I was little, I was the kid who took pride in hustling on my own newspaper route to take care of my customers and make some money. I also ran my own grass cutting business, and anything else that you can think of to make a buck.

If there was an opportunity, I took advantage of it, even if it meant sacrificing fun time with my friends. Whether I was cutting grass, shoveling driveways, or babysitting, I was hustling. I learned young, that nothing was going to ever be handed to me. I also learned two critically valuable lessons: 1) Opportunity is everywhere, and 2) I had no excuses.

While I was never truly jealous of others, I often found myself envious of the kids that had the nicer things while I had the hand me downs or did without. That really engrained into my head that if I wanted nice things like they had, I better go and get it.

I didn't know the word *entrepreneur* back in the day. I just wanted to make a buck, buy my candy (and some clothes or a new bike maybe), but I was budding into a businessman. Over the next few years, I was always hustling for some kind of business.

I DIDN'T KNOW THE WORD ENTREPRENEUR BACK IN THE DAY. I JUST WANTED TO MAKE A BUCK, BUY MY CANDY (AND SOME CLOTHES OR A NEW BIKE MAYBE), BUT I WAS BUDDING INTO A BUSINESSMAN. OVER THE NEXT FEW YEARS, I WAS ALWAYS HUSTLING FOR SOME KIND OF BUSINESS.

I'd discover mail scams that I thought were business opportunities, but my dad would luckily shoot me down. Like many, my parents believed that business and entrepreneurship were too risky, and that it was much better to go to college and get a safe (oxymoron) job.

Back in the late 80's and early 90's, entrepreneurship wasn't as cool and accepted as it is today. Where I came from people didn't just start a business and make it big. The most successful ones went to college, got a middle-class job, and often got out of Flint, MI. The adults in my life thought they were giving me good advice based on their life experiences. Okay, with the mail scams they did me a solid.

REBOOT—WHO DO YOU REALLY WANT TO BE?

Though parental and other advisors meant well, they never really took the time to understand how my brain worked or what drove me, let alone what inspired me. Working for someone else just sounded terrible to me, but creating my own businesses sounded amazing, even if there was tremendous risk.

They'd tell me things like, "This isn't the movies, David. You try that and you'll lose everything!" Or the infamous, "And, where are you going to get the money to start?"

So, here I was in 2001 with little to no formal education in a university or college, but with a back story that was indeed a PhD in the School of Hard Knocks. So far, all I'd done was proven those naysayers right, I was after all… bankrupt.

After my divorce and bankruptcy, I decided to simply reboot my life, just me and my baby girl. Tannah was my everything, and at her priceless age of four, I decided that she would be my only focus for the next 14-18 years. Only her and nothing else. I recall thinking to myself that I'd likely never remarry or even date until after she was an adult.

God had other plans.
With a ton of new life lessons to learn from and reflect on, still fairly young at age 25, my little girl looking up to me as if I was Superman, and a good paying job at the local telephone company, I knew that I could rebuild my life. I realized that God was using my bad decisions and poor choices to teach me valuable lessons that would carry me far. I was now a more confident adult than ever before.

I'm not real sure why, but concurrent to this shift in my thinking, I formed a tremendous interest to learn from my failed marriage. I devoured articles, books and blogs on the internet until late night, and woke early to continue before leaving for work. Truly, this subject matter was continuing education.

One day I stumbled upon a website called Match.com. I had never heard of online dating. I was curious and clicked on the link. I was fascinated by this site dedicated solely to helping people meet their match in relationships. I met and chatted with a few women, nice—but no. I'd learned a lot about myself in the last handful of years. While I wasn't really even looking for a relationship, I certainly wasn't looking to settle. I chose to be discerning and deliberate.

Did I mention God had a plan?

Well, inadvertently, I met a young lady named Carla, and was immediately knocked back on my socks. She was miraculous. She had an infectious smile, and a precious, almost naïve outlook on life. Even though she was a few years younger than me, she already had her bachelor's degree in accounting. We chatted some in the beginning, then more, then even more. About what? Anything. Everything.

After a few weeks of covering childhood to beliefs to worries to laughter, and even love, I was really intrigued by this incredibly well-spoken, educated and mature young lady. If I'm honest, I doubted it would go far given the fact that I basically saw myself as a failure, and she was well-positioned for life with a degree under her belt. I thought she was out of my league, yet true to form, I figured what could it hurt?

We eventually went on an in person (okay, real) date. It couldn't have gone better. She didn't seem to care that I didn't go to college. She was reasonably impressed by my middle class job at Cincinnati Bell. Maybe it helped that her recently retired father's career was at the telephone company, Cincinnati Bell.

On that first date, I acutely remember telling her, "I'm a fairly simple person. There are really only a few things that you need to know about me. First, I love my baby girl more than anything in the world. There's nothing that I wouldn't do for her. Oh, and someday, I will own my own business."

For Carla, prior to university graduation, her only focus was her degree. Now that she'd completed college, she was fully ready to think about her future. This included getting married and having kids.

Odd as it was, I'd always felt that being a single dad was "baggage" that most women wouldn't want. With Carla the opposite was true. I couldn't stop talking about my baby girl, was incredibly protective of her, and my life clearly revolved around her. In a strange way, that seemed to cause Carla to fall more in love with me, quicker.

Within a few months, we began to seriously discuss marriage. I suppose we were both in a perfect place in life for a mature relationship. We were married about a year later. Our wedding was perfect, and an endearing testament to our devotion to each other. Not only did I exchange vows with my Carla, but she also vowed to our daughter, Tannah, to love and cherish her as her own. Dad suggested this idea, Carla LOVED it, and I just cried…

During our honeymoon without the stress of our jobs and the daily must do's, Carla and I were able to connect even more. We both were intrigued by each other's thoughts, feelings, and—by all means, yes, our dreams. We each poured out our souls to one another in a way that was very powerful, emotional, and bonding in a remarkable way. Perhaps this is part of the reason for newlyweds going on a honeymoon, but the truth is, I'd never connected with another human like I did with her.

While on our honeymoon, Tannah stayed part of the time with my parents and part of the time with her mom. Missing her so much during that trip, we called her regularly just to check in. One day I remember handing the phone to Carla for her to speak to Tannah. While I'd observed this before, Carla spoke to Tannah as if she were her biological child. She clearly missed her in exactly the same way that I did, and that was just astonishing to me.

It was a joy to realize that someone who had only known this little girl for a year could possibly love her as much as I did, but it was true. Not that I needed any confirmation of my love for Carla, but that really sealed the deal. I'd quite possibly made the best decision of my life by marrying this amazing woman.

Shortly after returning home from our honeymoon, Carla shared her desire to get her Master's Degree in Education. She felt that teaching was her true calling. We'd moved into our new apartment, and were settling into our new family. We were fresh, young newlyweds who cherished having a 5 year old half of the days, sharing parenting with my ex-wife.

On the days that we had Tannah, life revolved around her. We went to parks, practiced fast-pitch softball (pleased to report that I am a coach in more ways than one), and we goofed off competing on board games. Monopoly was, of course, my fav. Tannah was one little girl spoiled with love and lessons, and Lord knows, attention.

On our other nights, Carla began taking her graduate courses, but it really meant the world to me that she always intentionally scheduled all of her classes on the nights that we didn't have Tannah, so that we could be together as a family when she was with us. That natural decision solidly reinforced that I'd married the right woman. Had she been a different person, she could've selfishly scheduled her classes for the nights that we had Tannah, and then had more "us" time. However, she did the opposite, she scheduled so that she'd be with her "family". This decision again cemented my love for Carla in a way that I still can't explain.

OWN THE GRIT WITHIN:

- *If you truly want to find happiness and success in life, don't settle for less than. Set your standards at a level that seems almost unachievable and don't ever, ever settle.*
- *Think about your hustling. Have you done enough to achieve your dream?*
- *Never…never…say never.*

Chapter 4

NORMAL - REDEFINED

"Normal is nothing more than a cycle on a washing machine."
—Whoopi Goldberg

*"As you move outside of your comfort zone, what was once the
unknown and frightening becomes your new normal."*
—Robin S. Sharma

So, there I was, in a matter of roughly 18 months, a broken, shattered, shell of a man who believed that I was a complete and total failure in life. Now in late 2004, at the age of 28, I'm at the best place that I've ever been in life, mostly because I'd refused to stay down. I'd refused to feel sorry for myself, I dusted myself off, cleaned myself up, learned from my past failures and had now made one of the best and most foundational decisions of my life, marrying a beautiful, intelligent woman who loved me for me, and who encouraged me to chase my dreams.

I'm not here to suggest that being married or even finding the right person to marry—who believes in you—is necessary for success, by any means. I'm very confident that had I not married Carla, I still would've found my way to success, mostly because I wanted it that bad. I'm also very confident that having her by my side just accelerated my confidence in myself and therefore accelerated my growth and ambitions. What can I say? I am blessed with a miraculous bonus!

After Carla completed her graduate school, she was now well on her way to her dream career of being a teacher. We were living in a nice, but modest apartment, and had paid for our cars.

Ready for my 'what's next'? YUP, change was upon us.

It was then that we had a foundational talk that I'll never forget.

THE TALK

One night over dinner, I brought up that I was serious about someday owning my own business. She agreed that this was important to me, and reassured me that she was supportive. We made the important decision that if owning a business were to ever happen, we needed to begin uber-preparing financially for that opportunity now. We discussed our lack of debt, modest lifestyle and our growing incomes from her teacher salary, and mine as currently a career-man, as a Cincinnati Bell lineman.

We decided to be patient and not travel the same road of our friends who bought very nice houses, new SUVs, and went on spending sprees that drastically impacted their lifestyles. A success tip that I now regularly give my coaching clients, and people that I mentor, is to keep your hand out of the cookie jar, as much and as often as you can! One of the biggest keys to success in life is delaying gratification. It is found over and over again in almost every success story.

Our decisions in our personal life would affect our long-term financial future. We decided that we were ready to move out of an apartment. We also agreed that now in our late 20's, adding to our family was important as well.

We organized a diligent and disciplined plan. We bought an affordable single-family home, kept our extremely modest (and not too costly) vacations, and plowed everything else that we had financially into our savings - or our... scratch that.... for *MY* dream of someday owning a business.

A COMPELLING STORY: OUR CAIDEN—A CADENCE

With that financial plan well underway, we talked babies. And, that we did. Sadly, we encountered tragedy by losing our first baby, Caiden. Caiden was a full term, healthy baby boy and we lost him a few days after his due date. Unfortunately, he'd become tangled in his umbilical cord and unknown to us, this ended his life before we could ever meet him.

While our first few years of marriage were like a fairytale, this brought us down to earth in a real way. Despite my experiences with tragedy and loss, I was completely devastated. My Carla was inconsolable, and that along with losing my own child, was a new low for me.

Unfortunately, my life of poverty had taught me that not only did bad things happen to good people. It taught me that they often happened to me. I lost my baby sister, Lisa, to brain cancer when she was only 14, and my brother, Danny, to lifelong drug addiction. I had experienced poverty, divorce, single parenthood, and bankruptcy.

Carla had not experienced the depths of previous tragedy or adversity such as mine. The truth is that nothing, and I mean *NOTHING*, prepares you for losing a child. We could have shattered. Instead, Carla and I held each other tight.

I knew that God and my family needed me to be strong. I reached down and found a level of grit that I'd never known that I had. God had prepared me for this moment and my Carla and

Tannah needed me, so I kept it all in. I tried to be the strong man that God wanted, and my family needed me, to be.

Of course, I had resentment creep in from time to time, and I was frankly tired of being strong, but we got through it together. Losing a child will change a person like few things in life will do, but again, I chose to allow this to make me stronger, rather than allow it to defeat or even define me.

After our baby Caiden's funeral, we were told to take our time to grieve and not to have another baby too soon. We tried to listen to the counselors, but ultimately, we didn't listen. We were in a healthy place and understood that Caiden couldn't be replaced. We decided to have another baby fairly soon, yet struggled to get pregnant again. We went to a fertility doctor at one point. However, they thought we just needed to "give it more time after our loss".

As Carla continued to struggle with the loss, she for the first time in her life, found the need to truly rely and lean on God. This led her to be baptized. Miraculously, that very night my second son, Madden, was conceived.

I think every parent will point to the birth of each and every child, as a special time in their lives. The joy, happiness, excitement and exhaustion are unique. In summer 2007, our baby Madden was born. Our Madden looked like me in almost every way and little did I know at the time, he'd grow up to be my spitting image and have a very similar personality as well. While he was a colicky, fussy baby who hated to sleep, he made me a better version of myself again, just like Tannah did. Solemnly, as did Caiden.

Never Stop Reaching

I now had 3 people counting on me. Never will I let them down.

Over the next few years, we enjoyed being parents together, raising our little girl and our baby boy. We were a family of four and it was the middle class, white picket fence dream that Carla and I always wanted.

AND, I never stopped researching and studying business.

While we diligently socked away savings each month, I continued to dive deeper and deeper into my dream of entrepreneurship. My job at Cincinnati Bell was status quo, and quickly wore thin with me. It's not that I didn't have a job with good pay and benefits, but at 30 years old, that was no longer enough. I wanted more for me, my family, and our lifestyle. I had reached a point where I needed more from my work than just money, job security and benefits.

I wanted to make a difference. My time became more and more valuable to me, and simply trading my time for money wasn't enough.

I needed more in order to give more, do more and be more.

ON THE LOOKOUT . . . WITH A KNOWLEDGE THIRST

Over the next few years, I was constantly on the lookout for business ideas or businesses for sale. Literally hundreds of times, I'd find an idea or business that piqued my interest and I'd pursue it. Sometimes within hours I'd poke holes in the plan, other times it'd take me weeks. I always reached a dead end. Something would tell me, it wasn't for me.

At this point, we only had about $15,000 in our savings account to use for a business. I was pretty limited. That's when I started to read and research terms like *leverage* and the difference in *good* debt, and *bad* debt. By my definition, good debt is used to purchase or build an asset that will not only generate enough income to pay for the debt itself, but it will also generate more income for my family.

To raise my game, I read, followed, and researched the likes of almost every financial personality, and plan out there. Among them were Suze Orman, Robert Kyosaki, David Bach, Tony Robbins, Grant Cardone and, Dave Ramsey—plus a plethora of others. We were debt free, except for our house, due to advice from people like Dave Ramsey. In fact to this day, if you're going to be an employee, and work for someone else for a living, then I recommend following the Dave Ramsey plan. It's conservative, yet solid advice for slowly building a reasonable nest egg for your family.

BY MY DEFINITION, GOOD DEBT IS USED TO PURCHASE OR BUILD AN ASSET THAT WILL NOT ONLY GENERATE ENOUGH INCOME TO PAY FOR THE DEBT ITSELF, BUT IT WILL ALSO GENERATE MORE INCOME FOR MY FAMILY.

And, if you want to negate the naysayers, Grant Cardone's philosophy of, "*If people aren't calling you crazy, you aren't doing enough.*"

I was in what I thought of as a good place financially. Since I'd been working my butt off since age 10, hooray for me! I'd cut lawns, shoveled driveways, delivered pizzas and newspapers, even hustled baseball cards and candy as a kid. Did I mention all of those hustles?

It is simply in my DNA to be an entrepreneur, but now I'd worked at Cincinnati Bell for almost 12 years, and I wanted something more. I'd spent the better part of a decade reading everything I could get my hands on about success, finance, the economy, and you guessed it, business. I was constantly researching business ideas, listening to podcasts, watching videos, and Lord help you, if I found out that you were either a business owner, an entrepreneur or even interested in these topics, I'd grab hold of you like a hound dog on the hunt, sniffing down any hole and up any tree.

I wanted to learn from anyone and everyone that would teach me. I'd learn from people's successes and also from their failures too. But one thing was very clear to me. I'd never learned from anywhere other than from real life Superheros - meaning already successful entrepreneurs and business owners. I realized that real knowledge and expertise comes from doing it in real life, not from theory, and almost always not in a classroom.

Of all of the experts that I studied and learned from, Robert Kyosaki and The Rich Dad Company have really stood out. I just cannot thank them enough for all that they do for the entrepreneurs of this world. I am eternally grateful for their educational company. People like Robert and Kim Kyosaki have literally made this kid from Flint, Michigan's dreams come true. Sure, I did the work, but they have given me the knowledge!

In fact, I estimate that I've learned something to do with business or finance from nearly 10,000 different people, most of whom I've never met and don't even realize how they've inspired and helped me to achieve my goals. This may sound completely crazy to you, but you might underestimate the obsessive nature of my personality and how badly I wanted this.

As Malcolm Gladwell writes in his bestselling book, *Outliers: The Story of Success,* "*Practice isn't the thing you do once you're good. It's the thing you do that makes you good.*"

AS MALCOLM GLADWELL WRITES IN HIS BESTSELLING BOOK, OUTLIERS: THE STORY OF SUC-CESS, "PRACTICE ISN'T THE THING YOU DO ONCE YOU'RE GOOD. IT'S THE THING YOU DO THAT MAKES YOU GOOD."

Let Me Give You a Why

This is why I'm writing this book. I'm writing this book because I know that there are millions of you out there just like me. You want it. You are thirsty for it. You want it really bad, and you're willing to do anything that's legal and ethical in order to get it done. This is the crux of an entrepreneur!

Knowing this—and being 'this'—is why I do business coaching and have built educational courses through my website (www.laundromat-millionaire.com). I've realized that I have a load of practical and useful information stored up in this overtly inquisitive brain of mine, and I'm now very passionate about helping and inspiring others in their journey, while continuing on mine.

Now tasked with finding *MY* business, I was as obsessive as ever! I finally reached a place in life where I felt I had enough foundational knowledge to get started because, unlike many people, I do not suffer from paralysis by analysis.

I'm well aware that the real learning starts when you start doing!

OWN THE GRIT WITHIN:

- *One of the biggest keys to success in life is delaying gratification. It is found over and over again, in almost every success story.*

- *Be obsessive! Entrepreneurship isn't for the faint of heart, and it's not for the pretenders. It's for those of us who are crazy enough to believe we can do it and will not stop until we do.*

- *You want it. You are thirsty for it. You want it really bad, and you're willing to do anything that's legal and ethical in order to get it done. This is the crux of an entrepreneur!*

SECTION 2

ARE YOU READY?

Chapter 5

NOTHING SEXY ABOUT A LAUNDROMAT? THINK AGAIN.

"Thus, what enables the wise sovereign and the good general to strike and conquer, and achieve things beyond the reach of ordinary men, is foreknowledge."
—Sun Tzu, The Art of War

I know that I'm ready. I mean, I'm really finally prepared to take this journey. I've spent most of my life studying and researching business and finance. I've now spent another 5 years financially preparing our family for when that opportunity arose, and I just cannot contain my enthusiasm.

To me entrepreneurship is like a game. It didn't matter to me at all what the product was, it was the game that I was most intrigued by...and I wanted to finally play!

IN THIS LIFETIME, YOU DON'T HAVE TO PROVE NOTHING TO NOBODY, EXCEPT YOURSELF. AND AFTER WHAT YOU'VE GONE THROUGH, IF YOU HAVEN'T DONE THAT BY NOW, IT AIN'T GONNA NEVER HAPPEN.
—DANIEL "RUDY" RUETIGER

With Carla now pregnant with another baby Menz, I was more driven than ever before. I was excited to play the game and was very driven and motivated by the ability to earn extra income, hopefully, eventually, semi-passive income, from it. I was (and still am) ready to make my dreams a reality by serving my community and meeting a need in our world.

Having grown up in poverty, I knew what it was like to be poor, really poor. I also knew what it was like to not be poor. Maybe not rich, but I now had a taste of the middle-class lifestyle and frankly, I wanted even more for my family.

Expand the Streams—Create the Flow

When studying the wealthy and entrepreneurship in general, I continuously found that the successful *NEVER* have one or even two, revenue streams. Success leaves clues. Do your homework. Study.

I consistently found that the more wealth someone had, typically the more revenue streams they had built. I wanted multiple revenue streams in addition to my job at Cincinnati Bell, but I knew it started with one. I needed to find a way to create a revenue stream outside of our proto-typical jobs (say it by letter - J.O.B.S), I didn't really care how big or small that revenue stream was going to be, I just knew it was time to get started on the journey. I knew that I'd learn as I went, and I'd learned that failure was the key to learning! Never be afraid of it. (But do know how to overcome it.)

SUCCESS LEAVES CLUES. DO YOUR HOMEWORK. STUDY.

As I read through the online classifieds on Craigslist month after month under the title *"Businesses for sale in Cincinnati, Ohio"*, I saw things like a landscaping company, a BBQ restaurant, a daycare, and then one day I saw it: *"Combination Business for sale in Amelia, Ohio: Laundromat & Tanning Salon. Two businesses in one!"*

Amelia, Ohio…that's where I lived since the 6th grade. Wait a second, I thought, I know exactly where this is! My heart immediately started racing, and the obsessive ambition that hides inside me at times came out like a lion. I imagine, for the hundredth time, Carla thought I was crazy but was also smart enough to just let me go with it.

GO I DID!
I wasn't at all interested in a tanning salon but a laundromat??? Now that was intriguing. It was intriguing to me because I'd read many times over that many self-made millionaires found niches in "unsexy" service type businesses. Additionally, these businesses weren't often things that many entrepreneurs were interested in pursuing. Primarily, because they didn't sound "sexy".

Would be entrepreneurs often aren't interested because of the stereotypes associated with laundromats, and others like sanitation companies, towing companies, auto mechanic, or even plumbing supply owner. In fact, over my years of looking at businesses for sale I'd seen many different models.

DISCOVERY OF THE SIDE HUSTLE

I eventually realized that with my limited capital, I'd likely need to find a business that could be run "on the side" of my corporate job, even if only temporarily. Laundromats and car washes seemed to hit the mark for me. I'd also read many times how these businesses can be a gold mine for a person who's full of grit and doesn't care about sexy. Luckily, a large percentage of people that are attracted to entrepreneurship, are attracted because it sounds exciting or impressive! Impressive and exciting…my definition differed. Laundry? Hmmm…I was instantly intrigued.

I jumped in my car and within 5 minutes I was standing inside this run down, dumpy, cesspool of a laundromat in Amelia, Ohio. She needed a facelift and my gut yelled to me that I am the one to smooth the wrinkles. Gotta say it—beauty is in the eye of the beholder. I just saw nothing but potential. As I stood in that Laundromat that day, I immediately pulled out my phone and called the ad.

A nice fellow answered the phone. "Hello?"

"Yes," I said, "I'm calling about your ad on Craigslist for the laundromat and tanning salon for sale in Amelia."

"Uh, ok. Oh yeah," he said.

"Um, is it still for sale? And, what can you tell me about it?" I asked.

The nice gentleman kinda stumbled through his words, but eventually gave some very generic information. He said things like, "It's a nice little business, but I'm just looking to move on. I don't live around here, so I'm just looking to sell them."

"Ok." I said. "I'm not really interested in the tanning salon, but would you be interested in separating the businesses and selling just the laundromat by itself?"

He paused for what seemed like an eternity…. "Well… Yeah. Yeah, I think that'd be ok, I guess."

"Great!" I replied. "I'm actually up here at the laundromat right now. Is there a time when we can meet up to discuss this in more detail?"

"Yes. Sure. How about next Tuesday? Would that work?" He asked.

"Perfect. Next Tuesday it is!"

I hung up my Motorola Razr flip phone and realized that I knew absolutely nothing about a laundromat, but I didn't care. I immediately drove home and told Carla all about this laundromat that I'd just looked at, and how it may be "the one".

Well, she was a little less than impressed with the idea to be honest. It went something simply like this:

"A laundromat?" she asked.

"Yup! I don't know for sure, but I'm going to spend some time and look into this."

"Oh… Ooo…kay…"

I could sense the apprehension in her voice, but it didn't matter. I was going to pursue this, and she was semi ok with it, I think. Obviously, she wasn't exactly crazy about the idea of us "risking everything" to buy a business, but she knew what she'd signed up for where I was concerned. I often joke with her that she just thought I'd "look" at businesses for sale as a hobby, but never actually buy anything. Well…let us continue.

Having a little under a week until my meeting with the owner, I just dug and dug like never before, into what a laundromat business was like. I found a lot of varied and conflicting information, but I kept plugging away.

The semi-passive nature of the business and the "unattended" business model were perfect for my situation—a situation which required flexibility. I knew whatever business that I bought, I likely couldn't just quit my job. I knew that it would have to be something that I could run on the side. Thus, my side hustle. Yet, little did I realize the real work and hours that would be required of me over the next few years!

SERENDIPITY?

I continued to research the laundromat industry, the local competitive landscape for laundromats, and met with anyone that would talk to me, including equipment distributors of commercial laundry equipment. Then one serendipitous day, I spoke by phone to a gentleman named Steve Millman at HM Company. I learned about Steve and HM by Googling commercial laundry equipment distributor in Cincinnati, Ohio. That night on the phone, I asked for an in person meeting and the sooner, the better. We agreed to meet at HM Company's office the very next day.

As it turned out, Steve and his brother are second generation business owners of their family business, which their dad spent his life building from ground zero. While Steve had attended college and received a business degree, he returned to HM Company to help, and eventually take over when his dad retired.

During our first meeting, I was immediately awash in his industry knowledge. I told him about my dreams to own a business. About all of my preparations. And, about this 3,000 square foot dump in Amelia, OH that I was thinking about buying.

"Amelia?!" he asked excitedly. "The building is right on the edge of town."

Steve knew exactly where it was. His family built the laundromat for the original owners in the late 80's. He immediately began describing the layout, the footprint, and every single machine in the store. I was blown away at his memory of the place.

To say that I was stunned by his expertise and knowledge of the industry, and specifically this store, was an understatement. Our 1-hour scheduled meeting turned into five hours before he had to lock the doors to HM Company to close for the evening. He didn't mind the time invested in our discussion. He was a self-professed *"Laundry Nerd"*, and really enjoyed talking shop with someone as enthusiastic as I was. He thanked me for coming in, and agreed to meet me the next week at the store for a site evaluation.

I left for home that evening at almost 8:00pm, and there was no doubt in my mind I had found one of the key pieces to my puzzle—an expert distributor. To boot, Steve was a principled, high character guy, which was very important to me. I could already envision us working really well together.

Guess what my next move was? Call my dear wife, of course. I was late for dinner, and she fully understood when I shared my discussion with Steve and caught the wafts of excitement. Diligence pays. I'd been led to discover the only missing piece I needed to make in realizing my business ownership dream and making it happen. The icing on the cake was access to great people in a great company, with the experience and expertise I didn't yet have, but would drastically need in order to be successful in this business.

Incredible…

OWN THE GRIT WITHIN:

- *Study—Success leaves clues. When studying the wealthy, and entre-preneurship in general, you will find that the successful NEVER have one or even two, revenue streams. If you have a job and want to be an owner, do your homework on what will work for you until your business is working for you.*

- *Simple—Ask a lot of questions. Make a lot of calls.*
- *Find smart and ambitious people who complement you well. Make them a part of your team.*

Chapter 6

THE GRIND BEGINS

"Grind while they rest. Study when they party.
You'll live like they dream."
—Grant Cardone, CEO, Cardone Capital, author, educator

When I got home that night following my meeting with Steve, I couldn't turn my brain off. After a quick dinner, I tucked Tannah into bed, and blazed into an ecstatic zone. Carla astutely realized that I was overcome with the enthusiasm of a kid at Christmas. Intelligently, she kissed me goodnight and went to bed.

AMONG THEIR MANY RESOURCES AVAILABLE TO MEMBERS, THE CLA HAS VIDEOS, WHITE PAPERS, NETWORKING EVENTS AND A BOOKSTORE WITH BOOKS ABOUT THE INDUSTRY.

Left to my obsessive devices, I was up all night! I was thinking, reading, taking notes and writing questions for Steve. At around 3am, I found a trade organization by the name of Coin Laundry Association (CLA). Among their many resources available to members, they had videos, white papers, networking events and a bookstore with books about the industry.

I whipped out my credit card, joined the organization, and doggedly ordered every single product that they had. I had been on a mission for knowledge and expertise, but now I realized that this laundromat was most likely the "it" that I'd been looking for.

I am admittedly possessed for information - as much as anyone could possibly be. And now, I could finally hone in on a specific niche. I'd literally wanted, studied for, worked toward, and dreamed of this moment for a surplus of 20 years, and it was coming true. I just knew it!

A few days later I received a large box from the CLA. It was everything I'd ordered during my late night laundromat biz binge. I started that evening watching the videos, reading the books, and even took the next day off work at my job to finish the material.

Although I was never a good student in school, I now knew what it was like to pull an "all-nighter" cram session. The difference? This was _all_ my choice. There were no tests tomorrow with a teacher in a classroom. I saw this as much more important. The free market - that is true capitalism. She was my teacher, and I was determined to be prepared.

After nearly 24 hours absent sleep, little eating, and completely consuming everything laundromats, I had completed everything purchased. While I would eventually go through each product a minimum of 2 more times, one specific resource stood out to me. It was a book titled, *Today's Coin Laundry.*

This book was a compilation of many different ent laundromat owners' knowledge and expertise, curated by the CLA into one - and it was epic. This book was a cliff note version of how to enter the laundromat industry and man, they didn't leave anything out. There was no fluff. It was page after page of practical, actionable, and useful informa-

YOU WILL FIND KINDLE AND PAPERBACK VERSIONS OF TODAY'S LAUNDROMAT ON AMAZON.

tion and resources unlike I'd ever read before. I quickly got out my pen and highlighter and went to town. Note: this book has been revised by the CLA and as of 2021 is now titled, *Today's Laundromat*.

As you can read in the Amazon description:

"Today's Laundromat is one of the primary sources that potential investors use to research the industry. Covering everything from inspecting an existing laundry to closing the deal, this book will guide you through basics of starting a self-service laundry. There are many sources available on starting a laundromat, but this book is written by the premier association for laundromat owners, the Coin Laundry Association, and provides a credible source of information provided by successful professionals in the industry."

PRACTICAL—WHEN ON PURPOSE

Part of the reason that I wasn't a good student at any level of schooling was because I often realized that a lot of the information taught in school wasn't deemed by me to be useful or practical. Additionally, I realized that no matter how hard I'd study, my poor memory would struggle to retain the information. Often the content was theory, not reality, and I was mostly tasked with memorizing simply for a test. That awareness instituted my traditional schooling shutdown. Because of this, I had poor grades, was often made fun of by the "smart kids," and was even mocked by teachers and parents.

Nowadays, I'd likely be labeled with a learning disability. But in the 80's, I was just labeled as lazy and stupid. I was told thousands of times in my life that if I didn't get better grades, I wouldn't get into college, and if I didn't get into college, then I'd be working fast food for the rest of my life.

While these things did hurt, they actually made me stronger.

Do Not—Do Not—Underestimate True Grit
While I graduated in the bottom third of my high school class and never completed more than a year of college courses, I always knew that I'd

find my way. I was steadfast in knowing people were underestimating me. They were underestimating my will, my grit, and my resolve to be successful. Perhaps in my younger days, I never knew how I'd do it, but I always knew that I'd blaze a path.

I estimate that I read the book, *Today's Coin Laundry*, a dozen times in the next few months. It became pertinent to memorize it all. Unlike in school, I recognized life is an open book test where we're allowed to "cheat". What I mean is that I didn't have to memorize. I could constantly refer to the book, and a plethora of other resources. I could also ask friends, acquaintances, mentors or even paid professionals for help. Not only was this "team game" mentality allowed in the real world, but it is common among the successful in nearly every aspect of life.

I learned that entrepreneurship and free enterprise do not care about memorization, or your singular abilities. What is cared about is your grit and that of your team, and the perpetuation of developing knowledge and experience. It often boils down to the wherewithal of having a bulldog perseverance to figure it out.

Failure is only temporary unless you choose to allow it to be permanent.

If you fail the test, no problem, just take it again tomorrow but with more experience and information. I learned that while failure in formal education is a permanent state according to most educators. Whereas, in the real world, failure is how we learn. As long as we get back up every time we're knocked down, then we will eventually pass the test. This realization was, and is to this day, a driving force behind my ambition. I now realize that failure is only temporary unless you choose to allow it to be permanent. In fact, I now fully believe that each failure simply means that I'm even more prepared for the next time.

> *"Success is not final, failure is not fatal:*
> *It is the courage to continue that counts."*
> —Winston Churchill

Let me take this moment to encourage you if I may. If you've ever been doubted, questioned, or told that you won't be successful in life, those people are idiots, plain and simple. They are only right if you allow them to be right, and that means that YOU have ALL of the power.

I'd love for you to take a moment, find that stubbornness inside of you, and channel it for good. Channel it for the betterment of society and your family. Those idiots can only have the power if you allow it. If you've stopped believing in yourself, please let me encourage you to take back your power and to go get it done!

SUCCESS IS NOT FINAL, FAILURE IS NOT FATAL: IT IS THE COURAGE TO CONTINUE THAT COUNTS."

– WINSTON CHURCHILL

BUSINESS LESSONS

Business lessons? The terrain and the gain.

Let me help you navigate said terrain.

OBTAIN A MENTOR OR COACH

Over the next few weeks, I was obsessed. Carla realized that something was different this time. I had read everything that I could, and I met in person with Steve Millman multiple times, and I called him daily. Speed dial has meaning, and I definitely had a need for speed.

With Steve's industry expertise, he confirmed what I was learning and reading and that the location in Amelia was, indeed, a great location. He validated that the competitors for this location didn't stand a chance if I did what I was intending to do.

As any great mentor can often do, Steve also identified which pieces of information that I was reading were garbage and could be pitched. While the internet and free resources can often be valuable, I estimate that 75% of the free information out there on laundromats is not accurate information or good advice. The good news is that means 25% of it is indeed solid, and Steve helped me to navigate this important process.

QUICK STORY/PERSPECTIVE

One of the best ways that I've found to separate the wheat from the chaff is to look for the heart behind the message. While there's nothing wrong with having a product to sell, if you look deep into a resource, you will find true intentions. Do they have a heart of a servant, or are they peddling a product? Do they truly care about others' well-being, or just making money? I'd point to the Rich Dad Company owned by Robert Kyosaki as a positive example. While they clearly have products to sell, they ultimately see themselves as an education company, and Robert and his wife Kim are on a mission. I personally believe it shows in everything that they do.

Another example is to look for commonalities in quality products. Find a great book from a great source like the CLA's *Today's Laundromat*. If that ends up being a solid resource (and from a non-profit trade organization to boot), then that organization is likely to be a great source of wisdom with their other products and services.

With a business plan formulating, and my learning curve lessening due to my accumulating knowledge, it was time to formalize an agreement with the current laundromat owner.

KNOW THE PAPERWORK

Letter of Intent (LOI): I contacted a business attorney, and he drafted a letter of intent (LOI) to purchase the business. While an LOI isn't legally binding, it formalizes a verbal agreement, something I've found psychologically locks in the deal in most people's minds.

Once we got the LOI signed, the owner agreed to hand over the financials for the business. I obviously had no idea what I was looking at, but Steve and my constant reading helped me understand things a little better.

FOR EXAMPLE:

Profit and Loss Statement (P&L): At the end of the day, a small business should have a balance sheet and a P&L statement. This statement is exactly what it sounds like. It basically states the businesses expenses and income, and concludes whether there's a profit or a loss. It's addition and subtraction, but oftentimes people overthink them.

The key here with any business P&L is to really know the business model and/or work with an experienced coach or mentor. You can nutshell the meaning of 'business model' to the answers regarding, "How does the business make money?" And, ascertain if this information is accurately and honestly reflected. Be sure you have the facts.

While addition and subtraction isn't difficult for most people, the truth is that it's very common in any business for the P&L to have misstated or conveniently left off information. The tricky part of reviewing a business P&L, especially for cash businesses, is that they either don't exist at all, or are totally made up numbers. Sometimes, they are flat out lies. Other times they are just "fudged" to make the business look more profitable than it is. Truth is, every single day, newbies overpay for businesses in all industries because they don't know what they don't know.

In fact, for the laundromat industry, it's also common for owners to conveniently "forget" certain expenses that someone not in the industry may miss. These expenses would be things like equipment maintenance and repairs, supplies, or even labor, believe it or not. Including vending income on a P&L, but not including vending Cost Of Goods Sold (COGS) is very common as well. Sometimes the owners aren't intentionally being deceiving. They just don't have good records. Other times, they intentionally leave off a few expenses and inflate the income, especially with a cash business like a laundromat. Skewing things a few thousand a month in either direction can easily cause a newbie to overpay for a business by six figures or more.

A QUICK STORY

Imagine if you will, a laundromat owner goes to sell his laundromat. He and his wife have owned the business, and lived on its income for 20 years now. The laundromat makes 115K per year in profit or Net Operating Income (NOI).

After further investigation, they really don't own a business. They own a job.

Let's dissect this a little more. They both work full time in the business, which is very common. She handles most of the cleaning, is the manager, and runs a drop off laundry service with maybe 1-2 part time employees. He handles all of the maintenance and repairs for the machines and the store, but neither of them takes a salary for their work. They just work for "free". They are content with trading their time for the income that it produces, but they really don't understand business.

In that scenario, if they were to actually pay themselves a reasonable market rate salary, and then add that to the payroll, then the business is actually not even profitable. The business isn't a viable business at all. Unfortunately, the current owners don't even understand this, because their business acumen is too low. Worse yet, these same business owners interact with other newbies in online groups, and other forums, and they tell them that this is normal and common. Scary to reveal, but at a 3-5X multiple, a newbie to the industry could easily pay $300-$500K for this "business" and quickly be in real trouble.

> In 20 years in the industry, they've never taken the time to learn business, just how to do laundry, and repair washers and dryers. In turn when they go to sell their business, they will value it as if it is making 115K per year. Now, unless they are going to continue to work for the new buyer for free, this profit margin will not be possible, and the buyer will have overpaid for the business at sale if he or she was not astute enough to study the P&L statement or obtain indepth knowledge of the current (or possible) business model.

You can see how this becomes a vicious cycle of servitude toward working *in* your business, instead of working *on* your business.

While this story above plays out almost every day in the small business world, it's actually much more common in the laundromat industry, and it's very sad. Oftentimes, it's why laundromats are given a negative reputation and fall into tremendous states of disrepair.

Success is predicated on education or lack thereof, and my mission with this book, our podcast, my coaching services, and my Laundromat Millionaire Academy courses is to minimize this behavior by teaching others. The end goal is to elevate the laundromat industry, and share skills across industries to encourage others' successes.

INVEST IN A BUSINESS COACH

Just think, there are likely tens of thousands of people out there in the world who've had this type of experience in the laundromat industry, and they actually believe that this is normal. They believe that there's no money to actually be made in laundromats and if you're not careful, you may just listen to them. Even worse yet, they believe that this is actually the correct way to run a laundromat business!

In addition to being a carnivore of all free information, or modestly priced information available, if you are new to the business (in any industry really) consider hiring a business coach. A great coach may cost you

$10-$15,000 or more, but they can protect you from making avoidable mistakes, and guide your way to greater success. View a hired coach or mentor, not as an expense, but as an investment or insurance against losses.

A laundromat coach should be an investment in your education. He or she should give you the ability to accelerate your education and therefore, your success. Additionally, they should be completely independent of any conflicts of interest whenever possible. I was incredibly blessed to have a mentor and distributor with the integrity and character of Steve Millman, a rarity indeed.

A big motivation for writing this book is to tell my story and hopefully inspire others to achieve greatness in the laundromat industry. It CAN be done! It's all predicated on understanding what you're buying and making sure the numbers work.

I went from a net worth of roughly 50K at age 33, to a net worth of 1.8 million at age 41. That's 8 years, and I did this almost exclusively with laundromats. While my goal is to educate others and keep tragedies like the above story from happening, it's also very important that there are more success stories coming out of our industry.

If done correctly and with the right motivation, the laundromat industry can make you very wealthy, while serving a huge need in your community. Please keep reading to learn how I accomplished this feat.

OWN THE GRIT WITHIN:

- *Depending on your starting point, you may need to work IN your business before you can work ON your business, just as I did.*
- *Remember though, that at some point you MUST commit to breaking this cycle or it will continuously self-perpetuate!*
- *Get a business coach. Pay them WHATEVER THEY ASK (within reason of course), and they will help to take you to a level that you are otherwise incapable of achieving on your own. Sounds crazy? It's not.*

Chapter 7

PLAN. PREP. OPERATE.

*"Someone's sitting in the shade today because
someone planted a tree a long time ago."*
—*Warren Buffett, investor*

There are many ways to run a laundromat and one of them is as an unattended laundromat. Owning an unattended laundromat simply means you have no employees manning the store. The customer comes in, pays to rent the machines, provides their own soap and labor, and then leaves when they're finished. The business owner in most unattended laundromats believes that they're selling a commodity.

Easy peasy, right? Well, not really. Ironically, most people have had a negative experience or two with an unattended laundromat and then assume that they are all run that way. (Thus, the need to elevate our industry!)

You see, someone still needs to clean the store, even if it's not done by a W-2 employee. Even in an unattended laundromat (which my first two stores were), there's still cleaning that's needed on a regular basis.

Let's not forget the cost of cleaning supplies. Often these are conveniently left off the P&L or the owner says, "I clean it myself." This is a red flag to watch out for and easily overlooked without the advice of a good coach or mentor, and continuous improvement of your business acumen. Whether a W-2 employee or a contractor, there should be line items and expenses for the cleaning of the store, even if the owners do it themselves.

A BUSINESS PLAN

In my studying, I'd always read and heard about needing a business plan and how important it is to have one. However, I didn't really understand the magnitude until much later.

With my first store, I really didn't know where to start. Luckily, *Today's Coin Laundry*, provided a very useful template for a laundromat business plan. I used it verbatim for my first store, the name of which I aptly changed from Hamlet to Queen City Laundry. I chose to pay homage to Cincinnati—known as The Queen City—the most fortuitous pick among her many nicknames, and not far from our Amelia, OH location. In time, the Amelia location would be known as QCL1.

I thought the document (business plan) itself was what was important, which it is. However, what is much more important is the exercise of completing it. Wherever it asked for specific information that I didn't have, I'd just leave it blank. Then I'd go gather that information, plug it in, and move on to the next step. This forced me to think about and find information that I would've otherwise disregarded.

Eventually, I modified the template dramatically to form the business plan that I use today. You can find this free template along with others on my website (www.laundromatmillionaire.com/templates).

This creation of a solid business plan requires you to research your competitors, conduct a competitor analysis, investigate expected or common expenses and, determine in what ways you will differentiate yourself from those competitors.

It is a tremendous exercise that I now do with every single new project.

Where's The Value?

After 5 days or so, I had completed a business plan for Queen City Laundry that included projections, expenses, and my plan for improving the business. It was time to again involve my mentor. In Steve's review of the plan, he thought it had real potential even though during my time of researching the market and reviewing the owner's P&L, I learned that the laundromat that I was looking at buying was actually losing money each month.

YIKES! It took me a minute to process this, because I'd always read the value of a business is ONLY in the Net Operating Income (NOI). I asked myself, "Why would someone be selling a business for 85K that was losing money? Point in fact, when I applied to US Bank for my first small business loan, they denied me. Their reasoning was, 1) I had no business experience, and 2) The business was losing money, so they told me not to buy it.

During that 'enlightening' 15-minute meeting with the US Bank loan officer, it was apparent that she was regurgitating the information she'd been fed by her underwriter. It was also glaringly obvious to me that neither of them had ever owned a business, and had likely never even known someone that owned a business.

Prior to getting to this point, and without my voracious appetite for learning and getting Steve's help, I would have been completely clueless myself. However, I was equipped to be a player in the business arena, not a puppet.

As reiterated earlier in *Laundromat Millionaire*, technical knowledge, in banking or other fields, is needed. Yet, practical business knowledge, instilled by great resources, foundationally reassured me. I think it reassured me because I thought to myself, well if the bankers don't have a clue what's going on, then this ol' boy originally from Flint, is about to light a match.

I spent about another week or so researching the local market, delving deeper, and spending a lot of time with Steve. I'd told him about US Bank denying me, but he encouraged me to try again. Maybe this time with a smaller community bank. I think he sensed that I was a little discouraged but prodded me. And after all, Carla had immaculate credit and despite my bankruptcy years earlier, my credit score was right at 735, which Equifax and others would tell you is in the 'very good' range, and darn close to excellent.

This reassured me that I was on the right track but all the while, I knew that if I didn't find financing for this purchase, the owner would eventually give up on me and find someone else to sell it to.

A QUICK STORY: KEEPING IT REAL

"Note to self and to you as my reader: Keep it real by seeking the good, bad and ugly from those who have —or are in the process of—experiencing what you are going through. This is where you'll find the real teachers."
—Dave Menz

In the true form of deepening our friendship and business relationship, Steve took me to meet a few of his customers that owned laundromats in the Cincinnati area. Now, these were REAL Teachers.

Like Steve, they were true entrepreneurs who understood how to value a business, and specifically a laundromat. They were doing it every single day, and had been for a couple decades in some cases. As much as I learned from books and other resources, I learned—hands down more - from a day of mentoring with Steve and his customers. I was no longer poking around to discover the secrets of the biz. I was downloading it from the noggins' that had been through it.

Admittedly, I had started to question whether this was the right purchase for me. My self-talk bit into me. Things like, "Maybe the banker was right." Even worse, "What if they gave me the loan but the business wasn't worth anything? Would I be overpaying for it?"

What if'ing is an anxiety builder eight ways to Sunday.

Time for an intervention with my thinking.

I brought my concerns to Steve's attention, and he quickly reassured me with his experience and knowledge that I wasn't overpaying for the business. I simply was not following my passion blindly. I was asking good questions of him, and soon would be asking others who'd walked a few miles in my boots.

They articulated details I had never considered. Steve and his customers explained how expensive necessities like water, sewer, construction, electric, and natural gas access are for laundromats, especially in some markets. They explained that because Queen City Laundry (QCL1) was in a great location and had been for 30 years (despite its declining without proper leadership), and that there is value in the location itself, as well as the existing infrastructure. That adds to the valuation in addition to NOI only, even if it was technically not making a profit.

In fact, there's *nothing* more important than having a great location. That alone was likely worth the 85K asking price. While certainly disgusting, old, dingy, dirty and frankly dangerous, this laundromat had been in business for years. While it was not profitable, it had an existing customer base, and it was generating around $1300 per week in gross revenue. There's also value there.

As we visited this laundromat many times over a week or so, Steve pointed out the good and bad equipment. "These are completely garbage machines," he'd say, as my stomach hit the floor. "However, these machines over here are very good machines, and still have life left in them with some TLC and a bit of servicing."

"Great", I said. "How will I do that? I don't know how to repair these things."

Steve quickly explained that HM Company had very experienced service technicians, and that they could get the machines humming rather quickly for us. When he told me, "Dave, if this place can do $1300 a week without most of the equipment working, just imagine what it'll do with everything working, let alone with some new equipment too."

That actually made complete sense to me since I'd seen the competitors and most of them were in worst shape than us.

Steve added, "Yes, there's a cost for our service calls. But if you want to learn, we will teach you how to repair them."

I picked my stomach up off the floor and found hope. And, if recollection serves, I softly replied, "Wow. That is amazing." My eyes held my sincere thank you, as I could see that Steve had the heart of a servant. That I am a benefactor of his deep caring...forever grateful I will be.

What I mean by Steve having a servant's heart is he has a heart that wants to help and serve others. His dad started their company from the ground up, and he'd built the entire business on the premise that if we *only* focus on helping our customers (laundromat owners) make money, by default we will make money as well.

His dad often told him, "Money… is only a way of keeping score."

Being a servant to doing good, offers the best service a business person can—and should—provide.

FULL STEAM AHEAD

Not really feeling completely great about the situation, I still didn't feel like I had a choice. I had to buy this place if at all possible, because I knew that I could make it into something better, and something that's profitable.

I'd already done enough homework to realize that there was a huge need in the community for a nice laundromat. Through weeks of diligence, and mentorship with Steve and others, I had reached the point where I was ready to give it my all.

Next step? I took a second crack at applying for a loan at a local bank. Bad news… they literally laughed at me.

Paraphrasing, and click off his remarks on your fingers, the banker said: "One, you have never owned a business. Two, it's currently the year 2009. Three, our economy is in the toilet. Four, you have very little money. Five, you want to buy this rundown laundromat that's losing money?"

With a muster of confidence I replied, "Yes sir. That is correct. You see, I know this area very well and I've done my homework. I've had a professional assess the situation, and he agrees that this is a good opportunity. I have no personal debt except for my house. My wife and I have a good income from our jobs, and…"

"Wait." He stopped me in my tracks. "Look, young man. I applaud your passion, but this isn't TV (which meant a 'get rich quick' infomercial I guess). Trust me, I'm doing you a favor and saving you from yourself. There's no way that I can approve this loan. You simply have no clue what you're getting yourself into."

Understatement - that rather rubbed me the wrong way.

ENTER THE HYENA IN A COMIC STRIP . . . AS BANKER MAN (AKA HYENA) LAUGHED HYSTERICALLY OUT LOUD.

THE HYENA CONTINUED, "SON, YOU ARE DOING PRETTY WELL WITH YOU AND YOUR WIFE'S JOBS. JUST STAY ON THE RIGHT TRACK, WORK HARD, AND YOU'LL BE FINE. I DON'T THINK YOU WANT TO TRY THE BUSINESS WORLD BECAUSE IT'LL EAT YOU ALIVE."

START THINKING OF THE DIALOG BALLOONS ABOVE OUR HEADS, AS IF IN THAT DANG COMIC STRIP:

I PAUSED FOR A MILLISECOND THINKING, "WAS HE RIGHT? MAYBE HE IS RIGHT."

THEN HE SAID IT. "I MEAN REALLY. DO YOU EVEN HAVE A COLLEGE DEGREE?"

<u>HYENA MEETS TASMANIAN DEVIL</u>

I LOOKED HIM RIGHT IN THE EYES, TOLD HIM WHERE TO GO (!@¢#~), AND ASSURED HIM THAT WHEN I WAS SUCCESSFUL, I'D NEVER USE HIS BANK FOR ANY SERVICES AGAIN. THERE, I THOUGHT. I TOLD HIM.

BUT AS I WALKED AWAY, I HEARD HIM LAUGH AND SAY TO HIMSELF, "I'LL TAKE THAT CHANCE LITTLE GUY".

<u>CURRENT DAY DIALOG BALLOON THAT SURELY WOULD BURST HIS BUBBLE:</u>

"WHO'S THE LITTLE GUY *NOW!*"

PERHAPS I SAVOR HIM EATING CROW.

Ownership

At this point, all 5'11" 250lbs of me was still fuming mad. I immediately went to my 1998 Honda Accord with over 150,000 miles, and it hit me. I'd come straight to the bank from work. I was a lineman at the local telephone company, which was hard work most days, and I wasn't the cleanest. In fact, I was filthy. It was obvious that I was a blue collar worker with no "education" and he'd just treated me like a complete dog.

I vowed right then and there that I would prove this prick wrong. Just like I would those teachers, and condescending classmates who got good grades and were going to college. Even my friends' parents all liked me as a person, but very few ever thought I was going anywhere in life. I was going to show them all. He had found my hot button and pushed it multiple times in a fruitless 30-minute meeting. He evoked smoke.

My turn to light the right fire!

Sitting in my car, filthy dirty from a hard day's work, I didn't know what else to do but to call Steve. Of course, he picked up on the first ring, like he almost always did.

"I'm pissed!" I said, and then proceeded to explain to him what had happened and that I'd now been rejected twice in a matter of a week or so.

He paused, and slowly said, "So, what are you going to do?"

I sat there for a minute and thought about it. Some pretty pivotal words in my life emerged. "Steve, if I have to apply to a thousand banks, I'm never going to give up! I've done my homework, I trust you and your experience, and I believe that this is the business that I've been preparing for and looking for over my entire life. I simply won't give up until someone says 'yes'."

Silence for a couple beats. I suspect he was smiling on the other end of the phone. Then, for the next 30 minutes Steve told me that the laundromat industry was full of people that took their opportunity for granted. He explained that most laundromat owners seemed to think that their business was there to serve them, rather than to serve their customers, and that I was different in that way.

Then he proceeded to tell me that in 24 years of working with laundromat owners, he hadn't met very many owners with as much enthusiasm for this business and business in general as I had. And, he was proud of me for keeping on keeping on.

Whoa... I'd just had two life altering conversations in a half hour. Some smug banker treated me like most people have in my life. He didn't get to know me. Just judged me by appearance. He basically said I didn't have a college degree, so therefore I wasn't capable of running a business. This turned over deep-rooted feelings and emotions in me that reignited an old fire that was simmering inside of me.

Then, directly afterward, someone I hardly knew, but that I had quickly learned to respect, did the complete opposite. Steve did something that not too many people in my life had done. He reassured me that he didn't underestimate me at all. Better yet, he told me that he saw something in me that virtually no one in my 33 years had ever seen.

Though I had always believed in my potential, it was just the reassurance I needed after such a blow. I think we all need someone to believe in us, and he did just that. He just paid this poor kid from Flint the ultimate compliment and he didn't even know it.

That day, I went from a pretty low, low, to a pretty high, high in a matter of one phone call. I sat there in my car that day and made three resolutions to myself:

1. I would forever be grateful and fiercely loyal to my friend, Steve Millman.
2. I'd apply to every bank on the planet before I'd give up this dream.
3. I would find a way to make someone else feel the way that Steve made me feel as he continuously believed in me. I'd pay it forward.

Again, I tell you as you read this - if you want this bad enough, then you can go get it. You've just got to keep going and never give up.

Ownership goes beyond the bill of sale. You have to own yourself too.

OWN THE GRIT WITHIN:

- *Learn from those who have been there. Put yourself in the way of them and find out what went wrong or right. Implement best practices and pay heed to decisions made.*
- *In life we will always have those who doubt us and those that praise and encourage us. Use the doubt, and disrespect as fuel for your soul.*
- *Surround yourself with the best in class, top of the industry (the Steve Millmans of the world).*

ON A MISSION - NEVER GIVE UP

"Never give up, for that is just the place and time that the tide will turn."
—Harriet Beecher Stowe

"Our greatest weakness lies in giving up. The most certain way to succeed is always to try just one more time."
—Thomas Edison

"You just can't beat the person WHO WON'T GIVE UP."
—Babe Ruth

"First and foremost: Dare to be a trailblazer, especially when it's easier not to be."
—Simone Biles, Olympic Gold Medalist, Gymnastics

"How long should you try? Until."
—Jim Rohn

"It always seems impossible until it's done."
—Nelson Mandela
www.success.com

DAVE'S CREDO

By now, you have noticed that this book contains a few common themes. At the very top of that list is this one:

NEVER GIVE UP.

If I followed societal or even behavioral rules, I may be—no, I would be—leading a different life.

If I had succumbed to criticism, I would feel like a lesser man, a lesser person.

When tragedy hit our family square between the eyes, we recovered from the bruises as best we could in order to forge forward.

I learned to learn my way, and rolled up my sleeves, burning the midnight oil day in and day out. There was no overnight success. There was grit—and a heck of a lot of it.

Love led the way. And as a Christian, I'd be remiss if I didn't acknowledge our God.

I was blessed with a servant's heart—the one created within me, and the ones granted to me.

The point is, I did not quit despite no's and naysayers.

The lessons I'm choosing to impart are a culmination of many of my own lessons so that YOU may travel a simpler path, even if it is the road less traveled.

Never give up. GRIT is largely a choice, it is a mentality. You can choose to have Grit or not. You can also learn to develop Grit. GRIT is a mindset!

SECTION 3
GROWTH

Chapter 8

OPEN OPPORTUNITY'S DOOR

"If somebody offers you an amazing opportunity but you are not sure you can do it, say yes—then learn how to do it later."
—Richard Branson

"If opportunity doesn't knock, build a door."
—Milton Berle

"Pursuing your passions makes you more interesting, and interesting people are enchanting."
—Guy Kawasaki

Moving along, I immediately began the process of completing the next loan application. In fact, I was no longer content with applying to one place, then waiting on an answer. I knew I needed to move faster, so I applied to probably 10 different banks that night. I was a mad man and

Carla thought I'd lost my mind. I suppose to some extent I had lost my mind, but I was a man on a mission.

Many times, we discussed the poor timing of *the one* (*my* business) making its appearance. After all, we had an 11 year old girl at home, a little boy who was now 2, and to add to the equation, Carla was 8 ½ months pregnant with our next baby boy. Have you ever lived with or been part of an experience with a very pregnant woman? She was miserable, overwhelmed, and frustrated with me at the same time. However, her support didn't waiver.

This buoyed my belief that when opportunity knocks, you either open the door or you don't. But, that opportunity may never come again. With this in mind, I just couldn't pass it up. My lifelong dream was staring me down.

Someone was going to lend me that money. They just didn't know it yet.

The Loan

If you have ever applied for a loan of any kind, you know there is paperwork. With some loans, there's a heck of a lot more paperwork than with others. Thus is the case, with a business loan.

Let's discuss what a business loan application looks like. Financial institutions require all of the standard things like, a credit application, personal financial statement (PFS), and many other types of documents in order to submit your application for review.

IF YOU'D LIKE TO RECEIVE MY FREE LAUNDROMAT BUSINESS PLAN TEMPLATE, VISIT MY WEBSITE WWW.LAUNDROMAT MILLIONAIRE.COM TEMPLATES AND DOWNLOAD IT THERE.

Possibly the most important document is the business plan. A business plan in its simplest form is a document that explains how you will run your business and generate revenue. A business plan in a more complex and proper form, illustrates a clear picture of your vision and how you'll implement it. A great business plan tells a story.

Little did I know that there was an art to writing a business plan but, I discovered (perhaps the hard way at first), that there was. While my first version wasn't necessarily ideal, I've learned how to properly tell my story. I recommend that you do the same. If you'd like to receive my free Laundromat Business Plan Template, visit my website www.laundromatmillionaire.com/templates and download it there.

To the many banks identified, I submitted my PFS (Personal Financial Statement), Credit Applications, Monthly Household Budget Statements, along with a bazillion other forms about the business that I was ramrod sure I was going to buy. Of course, as part of the package sent, I submitted my nicely written and well thought out business plan (that I was rather impressed with) as well.

I felt as prepared as I could be in my situation and was optimistic I'd receive financial approval. I was anxious to complete the purchase, turn around the business, and eventually allow this local laundromat to thrive in service to the community.

I was denied time after time by several financial institutions. While it took me a few months and probably 20-30 business loan applications that resulted in no dice, I eventually got smarter. I started calling in favors, and asking for help, then it occurred to me to apply to a local credit union through which I'd had several car loans over the years. They knew me as a person, rather than a number on an application, so I figured that might help.

Upon calling my contact there, I explained that I wanted to buy a business and needed a business loan. He responded differently than every other lender that I'd been to in the past 4 months. He said, "Yes", to my request for an in person meeting wherein I would explain my vision, answer all questions, and invite him—and his credit union—to be part of fulfilling a dream.

A few days later, I met with Mr. Neil Peterson at GE Credit Union in Cincinnati, Ohio and we chatted. I didn't tell him that I'd been turned down 20 times before, but with honesty and integrity I described my situation. I had my pitch down to a science. I brought a binder of documents, and I explained that I needed a small business loan.

"Awesome," he said. "We are currently trying to grow our business lending department and would love to see if we can get this done for you."

I sat back in my chair, mute for a moment, and thought, "He's optimistic. This guy actually wants to help me."

And, indeed he did.

SMALL BUSINESS ADMINISTRATION—ANOTHER AVENUE

A few days later he called me and explained that they couldn't make the loan happen through GE Credit Union. He was kind, respectful, and even said that he believed in me, but that the board of directors just felt it was too risky. Because he was so professional and kind, I took it well, and was respectful in return.

I was about ready to hang up, when he said, "But, if you'd be interested in working with us through the SBA (Small Business Administration), we think we may be able to get it done that way. Would you be interested?"

Now, there are many phrases I could write here as it might pertain to my answer. Something about what a bear does in the woods, etc., but I simply bellowed, "Absolutely!!"

This would not only be my first time going through the SBA loan process, but

THE SBA WORKS WITH LENDERS TO PROVIDE LOANS TO SMALL BUSINESSES. THE AGENCY DOESN'T LEND MONEY DIRECTLY TO SMALL BUSINESS OWNERS. INSTEAD, IT SETS GUIDELINES FOR LOANS MADE BY ITS PARTNERING LENDERS, COMMUNITY DEVELOPMENT ORGANIZATIONS, AND MICRO-LENDING INSTITUTIONS. THE SBA REDUCES RISK FOR LENDERS AND MAKES IT EASIER FOR THEM TO ACCESS CAPITAL. THAT MAKES IT EASIER FOR SMALL BUSINESSES TO GET LOANS. – WWW.SBA.GOV/ FUNDING-PROGRAMS/LOANS it would be a first for GE Credit Union as well. Known for being a lengthy, brutal process, GE didn't give up with the SBA or with me.

Then the call came from Neil and went to my voicemail, as it had been a long, hot and sweaty working day in the field. I phoned Neil back on my lunch break.

"Dave," he said, "We have an approval from the SBA, and I believe that my board will easily approve this with the SBA's backing."

Neil began to go through the terms, interest rates, payments, fees, and more. I never heard another word, and I didn't care.

I had a *YES* for the loan.

My dream was finally coming true.

They could've charged me 25% interest and I would've signed the papers. I thanked Neil, hung up the phone and literally cried tears of joy (much to the confusion and amusement of my coworkers).

I labored through my day's work, and the second I got in my car I called Steve Millman. He was over the moon excited for me, told me that he was proud of me, and then brought me back down to earth when he said, "Now it's time to really get to work."

After hanging up with Steve, I immediately called the owner of the laundromat and told him that we could likely close in the next 30 days. That info made two of us happy. I thanked him for hanging in there with me during this process and for being patient.

Of course next, I called Carla. She seemed stunned, but I think she pretended to be happy for me. Now almost 9 months pregnant, she was due very soon and the timing to initiate the grind of making the business a success, couldn't have been much worse. However, I never backed down, and gratefully, she never asked it of me. She understood that this was a part of who I was, and that this needed to happen.

A few months later in March of 2010, our sweet, baby Ray was born. Our little family was complete. There I sat in our birthing suite with our newborn baby sleeping in his crib, my beautiful wife exhausted from childbirth, excited guests coming and going by the hour and me in the corner, completing page after page of SBA paperwork in preparation for our closing.

A few trying weeks later, the kids with grandma, Carla and I held hands on the drive to the closing meeting at the credit union. She looked over at me and said, "You're really going to do this. Aren't you?" We laughed and I kept driving. No need to answer the question.

We signed mountains of *more* paperwork, and closed on the SBA loan for around $70,000. When I handed the former laundromat owner the check, he gave us a pile of keys. I'd become the proud owner of a dumpy laundromat in Amelia, Ohio. One that was losing money.

I'd done it. I'd accomplished a goal—a bonified dream - that I'd had since I was a little kid. I owned my own business.

Hold tight…in ensuing pages, you'll read that opportunity keeps knock, knock, knockin'.

OWN THE GRIT WITHIN:

- *When researching consistencies in human regrets at or near, the end of life, one consistency stands out. Research shows that people rarely regret chasing their dreams and failing or falling short, but they always have deep regrets for not ever chasing their dreams.*
- *Explore every avenue to persist and pursue.*
- *Whatever your dream, go chase it with everything that you have!*

Chapter 9

RAISING THE BAR ON STANDARDS

"Celebrate what you have accomplished, but raise the bar
a little higher each time you succeed."
—Mia Hamm, World Class Soccer Player

Since we'd had had plenty of time to plan, Steve met me at the laundro-mat the day after closing. He had parts in hand, new money boxes, and two service technicians to repair the equipment. We didn't leave until around 10pm, and by end of the next day, the awesome service team had nearly every machine running for the first time in probably five years.

We weren't alone as we worked, and the machines were not the only issues needing 'fixed'. With many visits before I became the owner, I knew the place was rather overrun with less than desirable characters who were doing drugs, selling drugs, begging for money, and just generally loitering in this unattended laundromat.

What I learned on closing day is that there was a homeless guy living in the store, with permission from the now former owner. He consid-ered him his onsite security. However, the transient's belongings were surrounded by drug paraphernalia in the backroom. This was another notch in the string of reasons unbecoming of a queen—a Queen City Laundry—that is.

What a mess, but onward…

If you are young or old as an aspiring entrepreneur, do note that your past jobs and what you learned in or from them can come in handy. Luckily for me, my former career as a bouncer at a local night club in Cincinnati, my rough upbringing in Flint, a lion-headed stubbornness, and a career as a telephone lineman, had perfectly positioned and trained me to remove riff raff.

It took consistent effort and a lot of late night runs to check the true security of the laundromat, I had to stand my ground after they threatened me and tried to intimidate me, but this was my dream. I was NOT playing around. Within a week of owning the place, the local bad guys had gotten the message. I think it helped that I was a fairly big, stocky guy who can deploy a fairly mean-looking face when required. They eventually disappeared.

With that obstacle behind me, it was time to get down to business in turning this place around. All of that due diligence pertaining to piles of paperwork, dubious humans, indefatigable studying (big word for me, eh?), and a passion to have it all pay off—it was the foundation for the new work about to begin.

I'd spent about 4-5 months preparing for this day. I'd done my homework. This included doing some honest spy work at some other laundromats around—and finding they were nicer than mine, but not for long in my mind or my patrons' experiences!

Plan the Work - Work the Plan

Having set up a great first month plan with Steve, and working around the clock, we made significant progress—and fast. We replaced or added proper signage inside and outside, did some minor remodeling. We painted the entire store, cleaned like crazy people, added a few big screen TV's, and yes, we repaired every single machine in the store.

The proof in raising the bar on laundromat standards, is in the fact that customers came up to me in tears more than once and told me that they'd never had everything working at once in this laundromat, and how much they appreciated everything I was doing to clean the place up. I appreciated the kind words and received them.

My customers would soon learn that I was just getting started!

A QUICK STORY

Having read that laundromats have a lot of lint build up in the vents, and that it is a serious fire hazard, I made them one of my top priorities. It didn't appear that my store's vents had been cleaned in decades, and I feared the condition of the entire system might set ablaze.

I hired a professional cleaning company to clean all of the dryer vents. They arrived a few days later with a pretty impressive pressurized system for cleaning the lint filled vents. This is an area (since unseen) which can often be overlooked by new laundromat owners.

Two days later, and our vents were nearly sparkling inside. They showed me the video of everything before and after, and I was stunned. The 8" vents servicing our dryers had been performing as 4" vents inside the duct, due to the highly flammable lint in there. I don't know how this place didn't burn to the ground, but I'm sure glad it didn't.

I shared the facts with Steve and he asked me how much lint they removed from my entire store. The answer? They removed thirteen, 55-gallon trash bags, full to the top with lint! We agreed that was a well spent $1500.

On to the continuation of the work needed to raise the bar—which meant a facelift on the inside, as well as a reputation lift in the community.

Transformation to Profit

While the store wasn't perfect, in a matter of about 6-8 weeks, we'd completed a total transformation of the store with merely our meager life savings and a lot of sweat equity. We even handed out thousands of flyers in the local neighborhood to advertise. Between that and the power of word of mouth, business began to pick up.

After about 3 months, instead of my rundown laundromat losing money, it was making a profit. To say I was relieved is a full on understatement. Starting this endeavor, I knew we faced the risk of literally bankrupting my young family right as we were trying to start our lives. Carla and I now knew we were at least safe from what I considered the worst case scenario, bankruptcy.

Now that the laundromat was actually making some money, Carla and I ran some numbers. Our sales had doubled. Yes, we'd spent a lot, but our plan was working. This initial success not only evoked a sigh of relief, but it breathed a fire in my belly.

I was motivated more than ever before.

FREE UP SOME TIME TO FAN THE FLAMES

For the first five months of operation, I'd stopped by our store every morning before going to my permanent job, at Cincinnati Bell. I'd stop again every evening after work to clean and straighten up.

As business picked up, this time spent became more of a task every week. I knew my time could be leveraged as more of an investment in our business. We hired a cleaner to take over this role, and were still making around $1500 per month in profit after servicing our business loan debt. In other words, this was our profit after expenses and debt. That was more than our house payment would have been, and I was only 33 years old.

Though some may be tempted to plateau at this point, content with achievement, this was when I began to dig in even more.

How did I choose to invest my newfound time? Frankly, one of my many secret sauces to success in laundromats is that I became obsessive about the business. Wait, I hear ya—okay, *more* obsessive. In a half year, I knew that I'd done some good things, but I had caught the bug. I wanted to learn and learn like never before.

As I excavated knowledge about our industry, I'd continuously tell Steve all about it. He'd either confirm or deny the validity of what I was reading. I was reminded of his intervention early on when he taught me that there is a plethora of bad information out there about business in general, but specifically about the laundromat business.

Another Talk…

One day, Steve and I had "The Talk". No, not *that* talk—I'd save that for my kids. But I did call Steve very animated.

"I'm making some money now, but every time I get everything working, it just breaks down again!"

Calmly he explained, "Dave, it's time to invest in new equipment."

With the business growing, my older and previously neglected equipment due to lack of use, could not keep up. Though he had never pressed me on it, he knew this day would come. And here I was, just now making money.

Always the mentor and coach, Steve consoled me by confirming I'd done all I could with what was there. If I wanted more growth, it was pertinent to continue to build and reinvest.

Having no idea what commercial laundry equipment cost, we began the discussion. I definitely needed to make a splash with some new 60lb commercial washers. Then he laid the cost on me along with other items he recommended.

Wait. Another 85k? Life savings—already invested. Experience with loans—definitely, invested. And, where/who would take me on this time?

Steve is patient and kind….and sensible.

The Making of a Millionaire...

Don't close this book yet. What Steve explained next, would literally make me a millionaire and it can do the same for you.

He showed me the data on what I should install and where. These would be my feature machines, and with marketing and people already talking about Queen City...they would attract more customers.

So...I asked, "How do I get the $85,000?"

His response? "The equipment will pay for itself!"

The skeptic in me immediately came out, as it began to sound like a used car salesman. However, Steve had earned my trust, so I listened, and here goes:

Purchase the equipment with 100% financing through the manufacturer. You get 90 days before your first payment is due, and by then the new equipment will have brought in enough new revenue to make the payment.

As I leaned in, he explained that in almost all cases, buying new commercial laundry equipment for your laundromat will pay for itself in three ways.

1. <u>Increased Gross Sales</u>. By adding new equipment, word will travel quickly that you have "Brand New Equipment" and along with your "New Owner" sign out front, people will come and check it out. When they see the new stuff, they'll stay, and your turns per day will drastically increase. Simply put, you'll get new customers.

2. <u>Increased Vend Price</u>. Since you're adding new machines, everyone will come, but they're also willing to pay more for brand new shiny machines. This will be just another bump to your revenue. This will come both in increased margins from your current customers, but also from your new customers as well. Extensive research has been done on this subject and it's com-

pletely reasonable to justify as much as a 20% increase in vend prices, even with the same size machines.

In our case, we were adding new larger capacity equipment which would act as a feature and market differentiator. We had machines that our competitors did not.

3. <u>Utility Savings</u>. As a laundromat owner, a big portion of our expenses are utility bills, and the old equipment is incredibly energy inefficient. By adding new equipment, even though your revenues will go up substantially, your expenses will actually go down as a percentage of sales in the process!

There's actually a #4 and a #5 that Steve didn't mention which are depreciation and amortization, but I'll leave your accountant to explain details. In short, you can not only buy the equipment with OPM or "other peoples' money", but then you can pay that loan back with pre-tax income from your business - AND you can depreciate the equipment so that a portion of your other income is tax free.

Steve may not have explained this at all, but I'm sure he understood it completely.

I was sold and after explanation to Carla, a smart, logical woman, together we embraced uncertainty and gave growth the greenlight.

We were terrified, and another $85,000 in debt we now were.

OWN THE GRIT WITHIN:

- *Invest in improvements, and you are investing in the return of profits.*
- *Customers will notice positive changes, and more customers will come. Be the vital resource they deserve.*
- *You don't have to have it all figured out, just continue moving forward one step at a time.*

Chapter 10

TRUST AND REALITY BITES
(THE GOOD KIND)

"I will be a man among men; and no longer a dreamer among shadows. Henceforth be mine a life of action and reality! I will work in my own sphere, nor wish it other than it is. This alone is health and happiness."
—Henry Wadsworth Longfellow

A month or so later trucks from HM Company Laundry Equipment in Cincinnati, Ohio arrived at our new Queen City Laundry in Amelia, Ohio with a load of new Huebsch equipment. Included were three brand new 60lb washers, twelve 20lb washers, two 45lb stack dryers, and three 30lb stack dryers. Within a few days, they professionally installed everything, and we were off to the races.

Within 60 days, our gross sales had increased from roughly $1300 a week to over $3000 a week in revenue. Among all of the renovations, new equipment, and new ownership, the community had really started to respond.

We were even able to raise our vend prices fairly substantially. Along with the increased revenue from the many new customers now coming to our store, we were able to make our first equipment note payment without any problem.

Steve was right, the equipment had paid for itself by the time the first payment was even due.

KEEP YOUR HAND OUT OF THE COOKIE JAR

At this point in our journey, we made a very important decision, and one we stuck to for years. The decision? KEEP YOUR HAND OUT OF THE COOKIE JAR! I can't emphasize enough the importance of this advice in helping you to grow your business.

When we made that first note payment so easily, it was a light bulb moment for me. I realized that if I stayed at my job and kept our lifestyle the same for a while, allowing us to continue to reinvest in the business, that the sky was the limit for what I could accomplish.

I also began to believe that if I found another laundromat or two, I could actually quit my Cincinnati Bell job and be a full-time business owner. All I had to do was stay the course, keep reinvesting as the business grew, keep learning from any credible resource that I could find, and keep my hand out of the cookie jar.

As usual, my litmus test was passing my thoughts by Steve who was very encouraging that this was indeed possible. At the same time, he tried to dial back my enthusiasm a bit. His intentions were good, and he was trying to protect me from myself.

Enter Bullheaded Dave = I Wasn't Having It

For the next few months, I was looking at laundromats all around Cincinnati in every corner that I could find. I eventually came across an old, run down laundromat in a strip center in Milford, Ohio, a 25-minute drive from our house. Not only was it in rough shape, it was no longer even operating. As I peeked through the windows, I saw all of the old equipment still in there, including green and orange dryers.

What most would call a complete dump, all I saw was a gold mine of potential, and a community in need of a modernized laundromat. Sitting there in the dark of this neglected strip center, I could already envision what I'd turn that "wanna be gem" into. I called Steve from the parking lot at 9pm that night and said, "I think I've found my next location."

As I told him about it, he couldn't help but agree that this could be perfect, especially in my financial situation. I had now been in the business for about 8 months, and my first laundromat was profitable, not by a little bit, but by quite a bit. We concluded - it was worth pursuing.

One thing I've always appreciated about Steve was that he never thought I was crazy, or if he did, he didn't mention it. He always appreciated my enthusiasm and passion for entrepreneurship and for my customers. In fact, he told me many times that most people in business don't share my passion, but even fewer share it in the laundromat industry. I'm sorry to say that I now know what he meant, as I've spoken with, and met thousands of laundromat owners all over the country.

My goal as I build out the Laundromat Millionaire platform is to inspire this same passion and standards for service and community, across our industry.

I call it "elevating our industry," but make no mistake, I'm not doing this alone. There are many wonderful people throughout our industry that share my vision and dream, and we're all rowing the boat together even if it may be upstream.

I've learned that the ones that'll be the most successful in our industry are the ones that share my thirst for knowledge, and a desire to serve their communities. I've also learned that things like passion and enthusiasm are contagious, and that's why I'm telling my story in this book. I honestly believe that the laundromat industry, when done well, is the best small business in America, if not the entire world!

As a matter of fact, one of my Laundromat Millionaire Business podcasts, focuses on The 7 Reasons Why the Laundromat Industry is the Best Small Business in America. Take a peek at it on my YouTube channel: https://www.youtube.com/c/LaundromatMillionaire It's available as an e-book too.

IN THE PURSUIT OF QUEEN CITY LAUNDRY #2 (QCL2)

With most of the due diligence already done for this area from my previous project in Amelia, I knew that I already had 75% of this pre-work licked because it was in a great location. Yes, the old saying is true, even in the laundromat business, location is vitally important. I knew that this was a great opportunity, so I dug in.

It took me awhile, but I eventually got the property owner's contact information and immediately called. I explained that I was "in the business" and interested in leasing the space with the old laundromat in it.

The property owner was rather excited, and he met me there the very next day, wherein I explained that the place needed a lot of work, but that if I could secure a long-term lease, then I might be willing to make the investment. He did not hide his enthusiasm.

This was where the negotiation began.

A Process to Success

Most amateur negotiators don't realize this, but the key to negotiating a commercial lease, or really anything in life, is to find out what the person on the other side of the table needs and wants. Some negotiators see this process as more of a leverage situation and try to bully people into what they want. They'll scream, cuss and even call them names, which seems rather counterproductive to me.

I've even known so called "expert negotiators" for hire who will do and say anything to get the landlord to sign. Once signature is achieved and check is in hand, they then cash their "consulting" check, and exit the equation. Before you hire some bozo like this, think this through for a minute. You, the laundromat owner, now are involved in a long-term relationship with someone who doesn't like you. Or worse, sees you as complete nincompoop thanks to your *consultant's* negotiating strategy.

Is that really how you want to start out a long-term business relationship? Trust me…. The answer is, "No, you don't." You want your landlord to see you as their partner, if at all possible.

In my opinion, the best negotiators stay flexible, respectful and they reverse engineer to find a true win/win situation. While I was a new business owner at this point in my life, I had a tremendous amount of high-level sales training and experience. Without even thinking about it, my training and instincts kicked in.

I immediately got the property owner talking about himself and his situation. I asked leading questions like, "Before I called, what were you planning to do with this space?"

He'd respond with things like, "I'm not really sure, but my partners are adamant about not spending any money on it."

Ahhh, I thought to myself: 1) I now know that he has partners, and 2) The partners are primarily focused on not spending money. I then would ask things like, "Where are your partners located?"

Here, I'm trying to learn if they're local (involved) or long distance (passive in most cases). Then, I'd ask if he was authorized to make all decisions on behalf of the group. I'm finding out whether these partners are a decision maker, or simply a property manager. Once I learned that he was the decision maker, I offered to take him to lunch across the street.

During lunch, I talked about my family and asked about his. There is a lot to gain in building a personal relationship with your landlord whether they realize it or not. I don't recommend doing this from a place of manipulation, but from a place of genuine interest.

It is worth time invested in these types of relationships for both the short term (lease negotiations), and the long-term (they could be my landlord for 30 years). As important as obtaining the right lease terms are, so is recognition that they are a person, a human being, and if you want to find tremendous success in life, you will develop a reputation of respect for others.

Never be a door mat, but be known for having a strong character and sense of integrity. Form your business (and personal) relationships on a foundation of mutual respect and trust. You most certainly don't want it on the back of a slick talking used car salesman that you hired to negotiate for you.

I ONLY RECOMMEND BRINGING THE CONVERSATION BACK TO NUMBERS AND BUSINESS ONCE YOU FEEL THAT YOU'VE SET THAT FOUNDATION FOR THE RELATIONSHIP.

After getting to know my possible landlord over lunch and touring the facility, I asked him what they were wanting for rent for this space. I only recommend bringing the conversation back to numbers and business once you feel that you've set that foundation for the relationship. Once I got the magic number, I let him know that I'd need to run some numbers, and that I'd be in touch.

I intentionally waited a few days, and then reached out with a few innocent questions. Things like, do you have the exact square footage of the space? Do you know how old the HVAC is? The roof? Are the neighbors on a long-term or short-term lease?

These questions are designed to accomplish two things. First, to let him know that I'm still interested. And second, to point out that I'm a true professional. Depending on the answers to these questions, it may also make him look at factors he hadn't thought about that impact rentability. For instance, an HVAC on its last leg makes a space less marketable and therefore, their rent amount may become more flexible.

After a week or so of back and forth, I asked for another in person meeting. At this meeting, I laid out my plan for the investment that I was prepared to make in their property. I pointed out not only what I'd be willing to do, but the costs. I wanted him to know and understand that

I needed a long-term commitment from him, but he'd be getting a long-term commitment from me in return.

I took the time to explain the value of having a modernized laundromat as an anchor tenant in the shopping center. At this juncture, I advise: do not do this in a patronizing way. Be professional about it. In other words, without saying it, I was telling him that I needed them to make some short-term sacrifices, but they'd pay off in the long-term and he would never be in this situation again with this space.

In many situations, you won't need to explain everything to the property owner, they'll already understand. Of course, there are also many situations where you will need to take the time to educate them, and it's worth the investment.

A QUICK STORY—MAKE THE NUMBERS WORK

I pushed him, and pushed hard at this point, asking for everything under the sun, but in a professional and thoughtful way. My ask?

✓ For all new HVAC units to be installed, but I agreed to handle all maintenance and repairs moving forward.
✓ A commitment to resealing the parking lot within 12 months.
✓ For rent abatements (free rent for a period of time).
✓ For Tenant Improvement (TI) allowance.

And…the checklist, with very respectful intention, went on…

After he picked up his jaw from the floor, I explained that I was a very reasonable person, but that we needed to find some common ground given the investment that I was making. Knowing that the partners' focus was not spending any money, I fully expected for him to balk at everything that involved spending.

My ultimate goals, of course, included obtaining a good amount of rent abatement, a reasonable monthly lease rate for the space, a long-term commitment with moderate increases, and to obtain everything inside the building completely for free. All of the other things were just a smokescreen, a means to an end if you will.

The great news is that because I took the time to get to know him, talk family, be respectful, and get him to emotionally commit to me taking over that space, I was now in the cat bird seat. I professionally let him know that I was willing to walk if I couldn't get the numbers to work, and I used that in my favor more than once.

He'd now seen that I was making a huge investment in his building, so he believed my numbers. Whenever, he'd balk at something that I really needed, I'd just simply blame the numbers.

"John, I'd love to be able to get this project going at X amount per month in rent, but the numbers just don't work." Then, I'd follow with things like, "I'll need to rerun my numbers, but maybe I could get away with X instead."

Now he's not negotiating with me, after all I'm his friend, he's negotiating with the numbers, and even though I made a counter-offer, I never actually committed to it. I simply said that "maybe" I could get away with......

Seal the Deal

Lastly, as my ace in the hole, I told him my closing line:

"Here's the thing, John. We've gotten to know each other pretty well, and you are the type of person that I enjoy doing business with. My numbers are really close, but I'm a little concerned that if I agreed to this just because I like you, that my business would eventually suffer. I don't want that, and as a property owner, I realize that your worst case scenario is a tenant with a business that's not making a profit. Since you are an experienced property owner, you understand that a tenant not making a profit isn't a tenant that pays you rent every month."

Every good "closer" has a closing line. The smart, and emotionally stable ones, don't make the closing line about themselves. It's always about the best interest of all parties involved.

A few months later I signed a 10-year lease, with two 10-year tenant options. A tenant option simply means a predetermined rent amount during these years but that the tenant, meaning me, has the right to exercise this option or not. I was excited about this as the lease rate per square foot for the area was very good, and would allow me to make a healthy profit.

Additionally, I'd negotiated rent abatement for 3 months after we opened the doors. Some people may think that's not a big deal, but occasionally these projects can go awry with inspectors. Having the abatement written in this way was a big deal for me. I found it valuable because I knew that my finances were going to be extremely tight. I needed some wiggle room when it came to time.

He balked at first, but after explaining what I'd need to do to get it profitable, he agreed. I was able to take over the space, as is, with keys in hand. For many business owners, this would've been an albatross.

For a laundromat owner, even if the place was dilapidated, there was a value add in every corner. You'd be shocked the value that you can find in things when you're on a budget. There's a tremendous value in the existing infrastructure alone in an older laundromat, but only to someone looking to revitalize the business. Of course, from the property owner's perspective to transition this space back into a white box that could be rented for any retail purpose, there would have been a tremendous expense for them as well.

In the end, the negotiation only took a few weeks and we ended with a truly win/win situation. The property owners got a great deal, and so did I. That's the way business transactions should always be.

WHAT DO I WANT YOU TO LEARN?

While I didn't have the education and knowledge that I have now, there's a few things that I'd like to draw your attention to in laundromat lease negotiations. First, as with any negotiation, the key to getting what you want, is to first find out what they want, then reverse engineer. Meaning, be clear on what you want, and play your cards to fulfill the needs or interests on both sides.

In the case of both negotiations for this new space, and our first location in Amelia, each property owner wanted the same thing. They wanted a tenant to pay a reasonable rent to them, and they wanted to make zero out of pocket investment into the process. This is very common and as small business owners, often on a limited budget, we must understand how to reverse engineer. What makes it worthwhile for them—as well as you?

While it never hurts to ask for the owner to contribute, some amateur negotiators start there and will walk away immediately if denied. They end up burning that bridge, simply because they don't understand how to truly negotiate.

Always remember, we're not selling or even buying a used car here, and you cannot approach it that way. Be a professional. Don't just jump on the phone and start making demands. Build a relationship that will last for a long time, and you'll constantly reap the rewards of this investment.

OWN THE GRIT WITHIN:

- *In this world there are many small-minded people who believe that in order for them to win, you must lose. If you find or encounter them, run for your life because they will suck you dry, my friend.*
- *Keep in mind, there's an entire world of people with an abundance mindset. They believe that we can find a win/win situation. That is what they're looking for in life. If you find a partner, teammate, landlord or even an employee with this mindset, then hold onto them, because they are golden.*
- *We cannot have too many golden people in our lives.*

Chapter 11

DILIGENCE AND MAKING IT WORK = FREE LAUNDROMAT

"Learning is not attained by chance.
It must be sought for with ardor and intelligence."
—Abigail Adams

I couldn't believe it but I signed the lease, got free rent indefinitely during renovations, three additional rent-free months after opening, *AND* we got everything inside the store for free! Wait a second. I just got a FREE laundromat? That's right, no deposit, no personal guarantee, and everything inside was mine on day one of signing the lease.

Before I pursued this location, I'd done a lot of homework and saw that the laws of supply and demand were greatly tilted in my favor. I realized that there weren't any decent laundromats around, so I went all in. Since I'd already seen this show before, I was even more mentally prepared this time, so I got to work. I had less cash on hand, but more knowledge and experience. I had some new obstacles with this project, but such is business—and life.

95

> ## QUICK STORY—NOW AND LATER ORIGINAL CHEWS
>
> YUP, I'm talking about candy. My homework on the laws of supply and demand started early, and the gears never stop turning. You see, I never stopped riding my bike to the store for candy, even once I'd moved to Cincinnati. I hit the local pharmacy which sold one of my favs—*Now and Later* candy. (If you haven't had one, you can get a stash on Amazon).
>
> I could get a pack of 6 for 10 cents. I'd buy a bunch. My friends—or observers—at school, would see me enjoying one. Being the budding entrepreneur, I said sure you can have one, that will be 25 cents. (Okay, I gave freebies to my true friends.)
>
> My rationale for the 25 cents was this: Our school lunch cost was about a buck seventy-five, and the kids had 25 cents leftover. Why not dessert? And, what did I do with my profits? Reinvested them. Eventually, the teachers caught on and I got a bit of a reprimand—at home and at school—but really? I was enterprising, even then.
>
> That was now and this is later…

FREE LAUNDROMAT

Within days of signing our lease, we pulled every washer except three out of the store. I didn't miss a beat to wave goodbye to them at the scrap yard. The dryers were old, but worked, so we removed the panels, cleaned them, and had the vent system professionally cleaned (e.g., no lint). To improve their appearance, we spray painted the orange and green dryers a bright white with appliance paint from Home Depot. Not the best, but they looked *waaayyy* better than before. And, they dried people's laundry much better after the vent cleaning. After sprucing up with new drywall, fresh paint, LED lighting, and a new tile floor the place looked pretty good!

As you've read, I'd just sunk every penny into my first store and had to fight for financing and the equipment within. In this case, the cosmetic changes at QCL2 (Queen City Laundry#2), were done with purely free labor, thanks to mine, and many others', sweat.

While many friends and family helped out here and there, my amazing father-in-law sacrificed more of his time to helping me than probably everyone combined. What can I say, I'm a lucky man to have in-laws like mine. They raised an amazing daughter and are two of the most supportive people that I know.

Almost all of those beautifying materials were bought on our credit card, and we used every penny of cash flow from QCL1 to—you guessed it—pay off as much debt as we could. We were still keen to not get our hands caught in the proverbial cookie jar.

Our equipment loan for QCL2 financed four 60lb washers, fifteen top loaders, two 45lb stack dryers, a few vending machines, folding tables, seating units and fifteen 20lb washers. After a ton of sweat equity and favors called in in every direction, we had made HUGE improvements.

I was completely whipped. Meanwhile, Carla had basically been a single mom for a year with our three kids, and I'd missed many aspects of the first year of my son Ray's life. That was and still is very tough to swallow, but I knew what I was pursuing, and Carla and I put one foot in front of the other, knowing the sacrifice that it would take.

This poor little kid from Flint, Michigan saw an opportunity to not just make a living but to actually shift and change the trajectory of generations of the Menz family.

Nothing would stop me. *Nothing…*

OPEN TO THE PUBLIC!

In early 2011, we opened the doors of QCL2 to the public. Even with my debt servicing, within 3 weeks this laundromat was also profitable. Within another 6 months, the store was really doing well. Despite this, Carla and I constantly talked about keeping our hands out of that daggone cookie jar, so to speak. We continued to live only off the income from our jobs, never taking money from the business.

I'd read about it and heard about it, and now had experienced first-hand that this is one of the keys to almost every success story out there. Delayed gratification. A powerful thing. Sounds easy enough? When it's your real life, it can be a lot tougher to do.

Let me indulge in a telling story…and it's not even mine… I like to think of it as a "lead us not into temptation"—type of story.

A QUICK STORY: THE MARSHMALLOW TEST

In 1972, Stanford University professor and psychologist, Walter Mischel, led a study on delayed gratification called The Marshmallow experiment. It was a very eye opening experiment in human nature and success.

In the study, a child was offered a choice between one small but immediate reward, or two small rewards if they waited for a period of time. During this time, the researcher left the room for about 15 minutes and then returned. The reward was either a marshmallow or a pretzel stick, depending on the child's preference.

Results varied among the children with some able to wait for an even better reward and others diving in immediately. More importantly though, in follow-up studies, the researchers found that children who were able to wait longer for the preferred rewards tended to have better life outcomes as measured by many different life measures.

Learn more at https://en.wikipedia.org/wiki/Stanford_marshmallow_experiment

---

My point with commentary on "keeping your hand out of the cookie jar," is that you can work very hard, and even work smart, but one of the best predictors of lifelong success is your ability to delay gratification.

Unfortunately, most people who find a little success immediately reward themselves by buying a new house, a new car or a nice vacation. Carla and I recognized that if we worked hard, worked smart AND delayed gratification, we could have greater long-term success. By reinvesting everything back into our businesses, we could accelerate their growth and health exponentially.

So that's what we did. Year after year.

AN INFINITE GAME: THE TIME FOR EMPLOYEES

Carla and I would work our full-time jobs, and live off of only our earned income, so we could grow our businesses more quickly. Everything the businesses made for the next 3-4 years was invested into other improvements to make the stores nicer and our staff stronger.

We saw our business model as playing an infinite game. As an infinite business owner, I make all decisions based on long-term viability, and improvement of our team and organization. This was and still is the guiding light to our decision making.

During this evolution in my businesses, I transitioned from running very profitable, unattended stores, into running very profitable partially attended stores. I did this by reinvesting a good portion of our cash flow in staffing, and finding rock star employees.

I hired store attendants, though the time it took to identify those 'rock stars', sat squarely with me as far as interviewing, training, management, and assessed performance. I realized that if I wanted to keep scaling, I'd need help beyond our store attendants. I also realized that I couldn't wait until I truly needed quality people who were adept at leveraging my time so I could continue to grow our overall enterprise.

I needed to invest in management.

One of the keys to scaling a small business is the ability and willingness to reinvest in your team *BEFORE* you need them. I've always seen this as making decisions today that will pay off in 2-3 years down the road. In my opinion, not making these investments ahead of time is often what stifles a small business's growth.

Over many months, I researched how small businesses find, attract, and retain layers of management, and I learned a lot. I learned that often our biggest strength and asset is in our personal network of friends, family, and their networks. I eventually reached out to a family friend named Marlene Adams, knowing that she could be the key to building a fantastic organization.

Marlene and I had been good friends in our younger years, but had both gotten married, had children, and grown apart. I reached out to her because I genuinely wanted to know how she was doing, and admittedly, I was hoping to recruit her to my team. I remembered her as high character and integrity, and an incredible work ethic. As I took a jaunt down memory lane, I realized that she'd be a perfect fit in my rapidly growing team.

I reached out to her, and we had many conversations over a few weeks. Ultimately, I was able to sell her on my dream and vision for my organization, and I explained that I wanted her to be my first manager/trainer. She was reluctant but eventually agreed to give it a try on a part time basis.

Having worked as a restaurant chain manager for many years, she was burned out and had become frustrated with the corporate structure and rules. I quickly taught her everything that I knew about ----- the operations of the business and months later, she took over as our manager.

Building a Team…and Greater Revenues

Within a couple months of starting our first location as a completely unattended laundromat, we transitioned to having attendants on duty for 4 hours in the evening each night from 5-9pm. By the time our QCL2 was profitable, we invested even more into attendants, adding a morning shift from 9am-1pm. It took a few years and bringing on Marlene to oversee things, but we finally reached a point where we were mostly attended each day at both stores.

Interestingly enough, we learned that every time we invested in additional staffing, our revenue and business increased within a few months, and left us more profitable than when we were unattended. Additionally, I found a better work/life balance because I didn't get as many calls from the stores, and our attendants were there to handle almost any situation.

In every month we kept our hands out of the cookie jar, we found that the businesses continued to be stronger and stronger in revenue, profitability and in our ability to scale. We were compounding, and our plan was working,

I had an "ah ha" moment. One that was key to my becoming a millionaire.

That epiphany? Whenever I reinvested in my businesses for really anything, the value that I was bringing to my customers increased. They showed their appreciation by telling others about us, and our business, again, increased.

THAT EPIPHANY? WHENEVER I REINVESTED IN MY BUSINESSES FOR REALLY ANYTHING, THE VALUE THAT I WAS BRINGING TO MY CUSTOMERS INCREASED. THEY SHOWED THEIR APPRECIATION BY TELLING OTHERS ABOUT US, AND OUR BUSINESS, AGAIN, INCREASED.

This was certifiable to me. My goal had always been to improve my stores and provide the community with a better and much needed service. However, if the money hadn't followed these improvements, it would have been tough to continue my efforts. I was constantly reminded of Steve's advice that came from his dad.

His dad would constantly tell him, "Steve, always do the right things for our customers, and the money will follow." While I never had the pleasure of meeting Sid Millman, I really appreciate that man. And, the son that he raised in Steve. What an amazing legacy to leave behind that has truly helped to make many dreams come true.

GRAVITATION TOWARD THE TOP

Constantly being obsessive about my business and my customers' experience, I also realized that my prices had stayed consistently in line with my competitors. As I networked and made friendships with others in the industry, I always gravitated toward those at the top of our industry.

That was where I wanted to be and who I wanted to learn from. Ironically enough, I learned that many of these top operators weren't out, or known, as a face of the industry. They were often quiet and behind the scenes people who just plugged away as the caped crusaders of our industry.

One conversation after another seemed to produce the same theme: Business is all about value, not price! These were scratch my chin moments of, "Wait, I thought…okay, so if I do this? Or maybe I could do that, and on and on."

In essence, I realized if I run an infinite organization and improve my businesses constantly (which was my nature anyway), then I would drive more customers to my stores. More customers increased my revenue, and I was also increasing the value proposition that I brought to the market. What I learned was that if my value proposition was much higher than my competitors, then my prices should reflect that and be higher. In fact, much higher.

> *Note: Okay, so maybe in that moment I became my own Super-hero. Really not my nature to wear a mask to hide my identity, but I was definitely creating a solid business and personal brand in my industry. Having a cape would be cool, but…I digress.*

At this point our businesses were generating some pretty decent income, even after all expenses and debt servicing was paid. There was definitely something reassuring to know if Carla or I lost our jobs, we'd still be ok.

Then it hit me like a lotto winner on a Gobstobber sugar high - I was approaching financial freedom.

Freedom, just say it out loud. ***Financial Freedom.***

However, let wisdom intercept. I knew that the longer that I delayed gratification and kept reinvesting, the more my success would be accelerated. Carla agreed, so we kept plugging away year after year. Every day, week, month and year, my focus remained the same:

Be better tomorrow than yesterday, in every aspect
of our businesses, and our life. Be infinite!

This nature of grit, was the foundation of exponential elevation in our brand, reputation, gross revenue, and our net operating income. And, our prices were honest and commensurate to the value proposition we offered to customers and our community.

I gotta pause for a minute here… and give thanks.

Okay, after 3 years of grinding, Steve said something very empowering to me one day. He said, "Do you realize if you keep at this for another 5-7 years, you'll be a millionaire?"

Whoa the ponies. What??? Knowing that I wanted to pursue more stores and knowing that I'd invest and reinvest into making them very nice, Steve realized the opportunity in front of me even before I did.

Giddyup…that conversation lit another fire in my belly like maybe never before. I needed to find my next location. So, I assessed what worked: I scoured for everything in the area. I found the perfect next location. Simple snag…The owner wasn't ready to sell. We had a good conversation, and I let him know if he ever decided to sell, I'd be interested in talking.

Coming up…delayed gratification meets negotiation.

OWN THE GRIT WITHIN:

- *Fear can be paralyzing if we let it overpower us. It can cause us to behave in irrational ways but more importantly, it can stunt our growth in life. If we let it, it can keep us from accomplishing our goals.*
- *I don't recommend recklessly ignoring your fear, but in most instances your fear is an illusion. It is False Evidence Appearing Real (FEAR)!*

- *Fear can also be a great teacher and motivator as well. Use fear to your advantage and don't let it control you!*

  "Inaction breeds doubt and fear. Action breeds confidence and courage. If you want to conquer fear, do not sit home and think about it. Go out and get busy."
  - Dale Carnegie

Chapter 12

SAVVY

"If you haven't found it yet, keep looking."
—Steve Jobs

At this point in my business journey, I'd networked with hundreds of amazing business owners in the laundromat industry and outside of it, and one thing constantly stood out to me. None of them were competing on price. They were competing over value or what is called value proposition.

There are many studies out there with the goal of researching what is important to consumers. In every case that I'm aware of, price is not typically in the top 5 and often not even in the top 10. So, my curiosity got the best of me again.

If price isn't as important to our customers, then what is?

Research has shown that things like convenience, safety, quality, cleanliness, customer service and many other things are more important than price. As I learned from my studies, and increased my own knowledge about consumer behavior, I came to the conclusion that price isn't even a relevant decision point in most cases. Additionally, it's even less important to the type of customer that I wished to attract to my laundromats. My expanding network of fellow laundromat owners suggested that the laundromat industry wasn't an aberration at all to this rule.

To be clear, this data was collected over many years by hundreds of laundromat owners, myself included, in nearly every market of the country. A big misconception in our industry is that laundromat customers only care about price and it just isn't true.

As I became enamored with this idea, I realized that it was even true for my mom and dad when we were very poor. My parents buying decisions were based on the overall value proposition, and even our local candy binges were based on the value proposition. We were much more interested in getting the best candy, than the cheapest, or even the biggest. I guess I learned more about Now and Later (remember my candy enterprise?).

Better now, than later.

VALUE PROPOSITION

This was a pivotal period for me in my life, and I think it will be in yours too if you put in the work. **Value proposition is EVERYTHING** in business, and I can directly point to this realization as another powerful moment in what made me into a millionaire.

Whether you're a laundromat owner or any other business, you must decide what type of clientele you're interested in. And, be very conscious about your decision making. If you make cheap decisions, even if you justify them as frugal, then you'll be forced to keep your prices low due to your value proposition.

If you constantly reinvest your time, resources, energy, and cash flow back into your business, you will eventually raise your value proposition and thus, your prices. Most customers can and will make this buying decision a priority, even when they're on a budget because it's important to them.

I've operated laundromats at the bottom of the industry, the middle of the industry, and at the top of the industry. I've also spent hundreds of hours with owners doing the same in these different categories. Regarding value proposition, I'll leave you with this tidbit of information—a gem if you will—which should be a constant reminder for us to pursue excellence:

> *The operators at the top of the industry have the best team, management, service to their community, personal lifestyle, AND are the most profitable, and this isn't even debatable.*

As time went by, I never wasted a minute, always studying, networking, building relationships and improving our value proposition. The more value in, the more value to the customer, the more value for the services provided.

FANTASTIC!

In 2014, our financial position and operational strength was approaching fantastic.

What is my definition of fantastic?

- ✓ We were grounded in our values and beliefs.
- ✓ We attained, cultivated, and cared for an exceptional team.
- ✓ We had not extended our hand into the cookie jar—we reinvested.
- ✓ We played a role in improving communities, and dare I say, people's lives.
- ✓ We kept on keepin' on.
- ✓ We loved each other, and what we were creating in our world.
- ✓ People were responding.

Could it be we were accomplishing our mission of the true grit it takes to elevate an industry? The Laundromat Industry?

In his book, *Greenlights*, Matthew McConaughey expresses many times his phrase, "Just keep livin'." He concludes his book with: *Greenlights. Here's to catching more of them. Just keep livin',* and he signed his name.

I appreciate that very much.

Livin' we continue to do, signed,

Dave Menz.

OPPORTUNITY KNOCKS

You may recall from an earlier chapter I mentioned that opportunity keeps knock, knock, knockin'. Now, when you read the words, *Opportunity Knocks*, know that it's not all butterflies and sunflowers or biscuits and gravy (you get the picture). Hard knocks come with the good knocking, and if that good knocking packs a wallup, well, ring that bell.

One day the laundromat owner phoned me, and simply said, "Ok, I'm ready to sell the laundromat."

"Great!" I replied with zilch hesitation. Opportunity was knocking, yet again. That simple snag of the owner not being ready to sell from our previous encounter, was about to dwindle.

At that point, I was still only looking to lease or buy the laundromat portion, but the intrigue grows bigger.

Time for talk.

Wash, Rinse, Repeat

Since I knew that I was mostly paying for opportunity, and I knew the industry well at this point, I didn't need to exert much extra energy in due diligence regarding the merits of the property. The place was in a smaller, 2400 square foot, standalone building and was in an amazing location. It was on the main thoroughfare in town. In fact, this stretch of road was one of the busiest business corridors in the entire state of Ohio. Additionally, it was located within 15 minutes of both of my other stores, and even closer to my house.

That is a 'lick my finger and stick it in the air' positive checkmark. However, and like my other gems had been, this property was very run down with little useful equipment. I knew it was a golden opportunity, but by this point, I'd also learned how to properly value a laundromat business. As I dug into the Net Operating Income and many other factors, I realized that it simply wasn't worth its asking price or really even close.

Despite my having some savvy and stronghold experiences in negotiation, we locked horns or were deadlocked over and over again. I didn't think it was going to happen. After many discussions with Steve and my attorney, Mike Barron, I realized that I'd be crazy to pass up this opportunity, even if it meant overpaying for the laundromat. With value add through the roof on this project, I swallowed my pride. After putting away the calculator, I made the decision to pay more than the data suggested that I should. My main reasoning was that the location was simply ideal.

A few days later, I called the property owner (a separate individual) to negotiate a new and long-term lease. He was a very nice, semi-retired gentleman, who I soon found out, had inherited this property free and clear from his father. His father had been a local real estate investor, but the son had no interest in commercial property. We talked and he eventually offered to sell me the entire building. I was elated! He was willing to sign us to a lease, but it was obvious that he really was interested in selling the building altogether. After taking the time to learn this about him, I made an offer that I thought would be a win-win for us both.

Since I was sinking every penny that I had into the laundromat business, I proposed to him the following: I offered him his full asking price for the property in exchange for 100% owner financing. I wouldn't negotiate or beat him up on price. This negotiation strategy is often called "your price, my terms" and it is used all over the world with great success.

I then explained that he'd get more money in mortgage and interest than he'd get in rent, but he didn't even care. What really mattered to him was that he'd be freed from the hassle of owning the property.

Additionally, I explained that his collateral (the building) would be safe, thus so would be his financing, because my plan was to drastically improve the building and the laundromat too. This would drastically raise the value of the property, but that didn't seem to resonate with him either.

What I knew he did care about was that in a few years I'd have significant equity in the property from my improvements, and would be in a position to free him from the building soon. I agreed to refinance and cash him out as soon as I had enough equity to borrow against.

Once again, this was all negotiated and agreed upon with nothing down.

In the end, this was another win-win situation. I was able to acquire a piece of commercial property with zero down, and save my cash to invest into the building and business improvements. He was able to off-load another of his dad's properties and free himself from what he saw as an unwanted burden.

While the building negotiation was fairly straight forward, the laundromat negotiation was more involved. Many people would've walked away, letting their stubbornness win-out but, man, am I glad that I didn't. In the end, my logical, business side won out rather than my emotional side, thanks to great advice from great mentors.

Queen City Laundry #3 (QCL3-Anderson) was about to be born.

A QUICK STORY- STUBBORN JUSTIFIED

Some of the best business advice that I've received was from my attorney, Mike Barron. Mike is a calm, cool, collected guy and frankly one of the smartest people that I've met. I'm so grateful to have such an experienced and knowledgeable man on my team.

His advice was fundamentally simple. "Dave, you have to take the emotions out of it. It's just business."

I quickly, and emotionally, retorted, "Mike, my businesses *ARE* emotional for me!"

To which he calmly replied, "Well, that's going to hurt you at some point and this may be it. Don't let your emotions dictate things. Let your knowledge, and experience dictate things."

WOW! I sat there stunned for a couple counts, because I knew that he was right, and I appreciated his candor. I talk often about how I've never been a very good listener when it comes to others. Oftentimes, my stubbornness kicks in and I won't listen.

Let me veer off in retrospect, to tell a story within a story...

I do not remember the specifics, but I evidently did something rude to or in front of my grandma Whitley when I was 3 years old. Mom took me to the bathroom and spanked me. She then asked me to apologize to Grandma.

Answer? No. Mom took me to the bathroom around 16 times to repeat the spank, the apology order, and to receive my 'no'. Even Grandma asked her to stop. In the end, Mom assures me to this day that I refused to apologize because I genuinely felt that I'd done nothing wrong.

Maybe I was in the wrong back then, and I certainly have the utmost respect for the matriarchs of my family, though I was resolute, and I still am. Maybe stubbornness is inherited or I feel it was born in me.

I'm in my mid-forties now, and if you tell me that I can't do something, I'll put myself in a corner (no reference to the movie, *Dirty Dancing*), and come out with a bellowing, "Watch me!" I'm no baby.

The one caveat though, is that I will listen, if you have my respect. However, I can be stingy with respect. You must earn it with me. Whether that is a product of my past or a success factor in my present, it's true.

> Providentially (YUP—had to search synonyms for that word), Mike had my respect so I calmed down and listened to his expert guidance.
>
> A shout out of thank you to Mike and Steve for their direction and astute advice.

INFORMED OPPORTUNITY

While some would say that I did overpay for the Anderson laundromat, I knew in my gut—and with my experience—that buying it was the right thing to do. There are opportunity costs as any business person knows, and there are also lost opportunities. I saw the price point as paying forward into what I knew the store would be—a success.

I encourage you to take this lesson to heart when placing a valuation on any laundromat, any business or under the auspices of possibility in location. Don't get too caught up in absolutes or opinion that could lead you to walk away from a lucrative opportunity. Net Operating Income (NOI) is important, but numbers are only part of the equation. Know your industry, do your homework, and make decisions based on the totality of information, not just the numbers.

Abundance vs. Scarcity and The Win-Win
In the book, *The 7 Habits of Highly Effective People*, Dr. Steven Covey, talks about habit number four, which I've always taken to heart and I recommend that you do to. I discussed Win-Win earlier, but I think it's worth discussing more here.

Habit #4 is "Think Win-Win". In the book he is quoted as saying, *"When one side benefits more than the other, that's a win-lose situation. To the winner it might look like success for a while, but in the long run, it breeds resentment and distrust."*

Dr. Covey continues, *"Think Win-Win. It isn't about being nice, weak, nor is it a quick-fix technique. It is a character-based code for human interaction and collaboration."*

Stop for a second and process that. Read that last sentence again a few more times and really let that sink in.

The quote continues:

"Most of us learn to base our self-worth on comparisons and competition. We think about succeeding in terms of someone else failing-that is, if I win, you lose; or if you win, I lose. Life becomes a zero-sum game. There is only so much pie to go around, and if you get a big piece, there is less for me; It's not fair, and I'm going to make sure you don't get anymore. We all play the game, but how much fun is it really?"

As Dr. Covey stated so eloquently, there are two ways to look at our businesses, the transactions we enter into, and for that matter our lives. One is a zero-sum game, where there's a limited amount of pie. This mindset is often referred to as the "Scarcity Mindset." The other is where the pie gets bigger and bigger, which is often referred to as an "Abundance Mindset".

I credit my abundance mindset to a large portion of my success, and I have seen many situations where a scarcity mindset comes back to bite people later on. However, I don't believe in these things because they somehow get me ahead in life, I believe in them because this is who I am to my core.

My faith and my upbringing taught me to serve others, rather than use them only for bettering myself and my family. To be clear, people didn't teach me this, GOD DID. I certainly did have some great people in my life that reinforced it. I'm now eternally grateful for those lessons early on in my life and they continue to serve me well. It also allows me to sleep peacefully at night knowing that for every accomplishment I've

HABIT #4 IS "THINK WIN-WIN". IN THE BOOK HE IS QUOTED AS SAYING, "WHEN ONE SIDE BENEFITS MORE THAN THE OTHER, THAT'S A WIN-LOSE SITUATION. TO THE WINNER IT MIGHT LOOK LIKE SUCCESS FOR A WHILE, BUT IN THE LONG RUN, IT BREEDS RESENTMENT AND DISTRUST."

found in my life, someone else has won too. That is the way life, success, and true capitalism is designed to work, and frankly, how they work best!

The interesting thing about the negotiation for the Anderson, OH building is that my abundance mindset and win-win attitude, probably allowed me to buy my first piece of commercial property with no money down. As I have discussions with others, including the sellers, I'm always trying to figure out how I can help them, and/or what their motivation is.

I'M NOT LOOKING TO MANIPULATE ANYONE, I'M GENUINELY INTERESTED IN WHAT'S IMPORTANT TO THEM, AND I GENUINELY WANT TO HELP THEM WIN.

I'm not looking to manipulate anyone, I'm genuinely interested in what's important to them, and I genuinely want to help them win.

The deal worked perfectly for all and we acquired the property and business with zero down on the building and very little down on the business. I was absolutely over the moon! This allowed me to acquire two fantastic assets, rather than one, and control my business's rent and property management myself.

I could also rest very well at night knowing that I didn't screw someone over to get ahead. I suspect if I talked to this gentleman today, he'd still speak highly of me, and be very happy with the deal he made. We invested heavily and quickly and within about 4 years, we refinanced the building, paid him in full, pulled some cash equity out of the property and everyone was happy.

This project, the creativity needed for financing, renovations and more, was life altering for me. I now more specifically realized that I wasn't limited by my cash or my debt. I was only limited by my character, my reputation, and my creativity—which were all deemed to be in pretty good shape—and, I was well on my way to becoming a millionaire.

Ironically, as of the writing of this book, I used this exact strategy again in order to purchase a much bigger and eventually more profitable piece of property. This 1.7 acre piece of prime commercial property was achieved as another win/win situation. While these types of situations aren't everywhere, they are out there, but they require everything I've mentioned so far.

Also remember… you can't fake it. You must find a true win/win.

OWN THE GRIT WITHIN:

- *Sometimes in life, you can do things the right way. You can make all the right moves, decisions and sacrifices and the reality is that you are still not guaranteed anything.*
- *When opportunity knocks, be informed, and knock back.*
- *And, I still maintain, NEVER. GIVE. UP!*

Chapter 13

THE PIVOT—ELEVATING AN INDUSTRY

"Before a dream can mature and manifest itself as real,
a lot of loaded efforts come into play! You are the pivot
on which those loads must be turned!"
—Israelmore Ayivor, Shaping the Dream

RING THE BELL

After enduring all of the sacrifice and delayed gratification, we now realized that we were finally in a position for me to leave my job at Cincinnati Bell.

I had a good career with them and am grateful, though this time, the ringing in my ears was that of a jubilant chorus chiming of accomplishment. I resigned and was able to fully focus on my businesses for the first time.

Now having our first commercial property and a third laundromat in our portfolio, I realized that the future was bright, and if I'm honest, I had to pinch myself at times. I mean seriously, I would have never dreamed that I could accomplish the things that I was accomplishing. Yet, here I was!

At the same time as I left my job at Cincinnati Bell, we also promoted our manager, Marlene, to General Manager of the company. We began placing store managers under her supervision. Between not having my corporate job to distract me anymore and promoting Marlene, I realized that these decisions had raised our ceiling to a level that I'd never dreamed. Carla, Marlene and I, now each being roughly 39 years old, would be able to move faster and accomplish more than ever before.

Within days of closing on QCL3 Anderson, we'd begun the remodel and ordered the first phase of new equipment. While this location was in poor condition, we were pleasantly surprised to find that a good portion of the equipment was in reasonably good shape. We replaced about 50% of the equipment in the store all at one time, and continued our full renovation of the store. This included new bulkheads, new ceilings, LED lighting, TV's, porcelain tile floors, doors, paint, new changer, 45lb stack dryers, 80lb washers, 60lb washers, and 30lb stack dryers—and that was just the beginning!

With these renovations in full swing, it was really time to expand our business model. This would include expanding services our patrons still needed and would use.

We could bridge a gap.

THE QUEEN CITY LAUNDRY PIVOT

In the Forbes article, *How to Pivot Successfully in Business*, by Vikas Agrawal, the pivot is described as follows: "While pivoting a business can breathe new life into an otherwise failing business, it also means you have to start from scratch and abandon all the investments that you had previously put into your company."

Well, we were not failing at Queen City Laundry, not in any of our stores, in fact they were thriving. Yet, were we doing all we could do and being all that we could be? Was I striding forward in my mission to actually elevate an industry? Was I thinking big enough?

If you read on in the Forbes article, you will find: *"A pivot means fundamentally changing the direction of a business when you realize the current products or services aren't meeting the needs of the market. The main goal of a pivot is to help a company improve revenue or survive in the market, but the way you pivot your business can make all the difference."*

Ding, ding ding!! Ahhh….so, the market we serve may have, or likely has, additional needs that we can provide as a vital community service. That's how the Queen City Laundry team came to think of our pivot.

Our pivot was a full on expansion of our thinking, business practices and our service offerings. While entirely successful in running unattended laundromats, we saw more potential and opportunity in "pivoting" away from the unattended model and into a full service model.

Steadfast in all, would be our mission to lean into the elite side of what it meant to be an owner, and create happy customers and increasing profits. All the while, the pivot we chose to create, is literally elevating the Laundromat Industry.

UPSCALING THE BUSINESS MODEL - BIG PICTURE THINKING

We were not completely new to the laundromat industry, but there was a lot more to learn—then integrate into our business model, and our operations.

I started delving into the other business models of our industry, specifically focusing on the viability of adding drop off laundry as an additional income stream. Besides helping me to make an educated choice to expand our business model, my research helped me gain much more than just that.

After reading, networking, and building genuine friendships with the top operators

DON'T FOCUS ON THE LITTLE DETAILS AND EXPENSES. INSTEAD, FOCUS ON - NO OBSESS ABOUT - THE MACRO! THE BIG MINDED, BIG PICTURE THINKING. PLAY THE LONG GAME.

in the laundromat industry, I'd learned some very valuable lessons. I'd learned that thinking long-term is almost always the best strategy, so that's what I'd begun to do.

From that point forward, I'd decided that every decision we made as a business would be based on where we wanted to be 3-5 years out. If you're looking for a tip or secret sauce for running any business, here's one for you:

> *Don't focus on the little details and expenses. Instead, focus on*
> *- no OBSESS about - the macro! The big minded,*
> *big picture thinking. Play the long game. Think infinite.*

I'm not suggesting that the details don't add up when it comes to your value proposition, because they do. But, I've seen business owners obsess over their utilities, their payroll and even being debt free. Wrong obsessions! This is small-minded thinking when it comes to business.

This type of thinking will gain you a small amount of success, but if you want much bigger success, then you must obsess and plan for 3-5 years out, and that almost always requires keeping your hand outta that cookie jar! And, of course, by cookies, I mean keep your eye on your endgame, which I'll rinse and repeat—it requires sacrifice and delayed gratification. I'll add to it. It requires you to be forward thinking. What's that old adage? Oh yeah, 'do what you always did, get what ya always got'.

EXPANSION OF SERVICES (AND THEREFORE, VALUE)

Having learned with my first two stores that *"pivoting"* from unattended to partially attended (and eventually fully attended) stores had improved customer service and our overall value proposition, I decided around year three of our journey to dig deeper. I felt a need to discover more options. And, based on my discoveries more vetted decision-making was to come.

One of these options presented itself shortly after buying QCL3 (Anderson). The store was already partially attended, but also had a Drop

Off Laundry service. I'd read and learned a little something about this over the years, but really had very little knowledge. Drop off laundry fills a need, but unfortunately, the service at this store was very poorly managed. The finished product was certainly nothing to write home about.

A QUICK LESSON—KEEP YOUR EYE ON THE PRIZE AND DON'T SWEAT THE SMALL STUFF

I'm quickly reminded to keep my eye on the prize every time I hear a discussion about irrelevant things, such as the cost of hangers or the price of natural gas. I'm not suggesting that we shouldn't shop these things or seek reasonable pricing. I'm simply suggesting that a good portion of the laundromat industry obsesses over these things, and that is not a good use of time.

One of the biggest complaints among laundromat owners in the industry is the difficulty in attracting, training, and retaining a great team. Just imagine, if every hour that we spent focusing on the little things, we spent obsessed over our team members and our company culture. Our value proposition, and therefore our prices would go up exponentially! In the case of most top operators, this renders the cost of natural gas a moot point.

Over the years, I've begun to refer to this vision and execution of the macro (big picture), as working ON your business rather than IN it. (Thanks to the book *E-Myth Revisited* by Michael Gerber.) Oftentimes in a small business, we must balance doing both, but I encourage all business owners to always defer to the macro rather than the micro. This is big picture stuff, and yes, once we get the big picture stuff down to a science, then we move to the little details.

If you're obsessed with focusing on small stuff like your utilities as a percentage of sales, you may miss the fact that your vend prices are too low.

If you're obsessed with how many years you can squeeze out of your 20 year old equipment, then you may miss that the industry is passing you by with modernized technology, tools, and features.

If you're obsessed with your budget and profit margins, then you may miss the fact that your rival stores are reinvesting, and leaving you in the dust.

Another example is focusing on your payroll as a percentage of sales, but then wondering why your team isn't stronger.

The point is, the decisions in any business model improvement can be a 'what comes first, the chicken or the egg', type of scenario. Once you've fine-tuned the big picture things, then you can focus on improving the smaller details, and this can fine tune your operations as well.

I caution you, though, not to ever lose track of the macro because that is what really matters.

STUDY THE POOR OPERATORS AND STUDY THE ELITE

Over the years, I've consistently learned that the operators in the bottom of the industry, hesitate to raise their vend prices, struggle with repeatable processes, often have outdated equipment, amenities and lack solid management and a scalability plan. This is often a detriment to a business's future because they spend all of their time on the little stuff. These owners think nothing of spending hours a day fixing their own equipment to save a buck or two.

AND THAT'S JUST NOT HOW EDUCATION AND KNOWLEDGE WORKS. IT'S PROGRESSIVE.

I'll recap this: In short, they're shortsightedness causes them to constantly work IN their business when they should be working ON their business.

You know the type… These are those laundromat owners that pride themselves on having 30-40 year old equipment that is "still running just fine." If this is you, I'm not here to judge or denigrate you, I'm here to offer you a lifeline. You can do better by yourself and your family.

I've always believed that we learn best from observing and studying others, and that includes those that operate poorly. Want to learn what NOT to do? Observe those that are not at the top of their industry. Observe the ones that make excuses rather than achieve results. And, the ones that have a justification for everything rather than ever considering the idea that they could possibly be doing something wrong.

Sometimes our choices are simply due to bad info in, bad info out—and therefore, bad results. You will recall from prior chapters that some of what you read in laundry literature is accurate, and some of it is definitely not. Avoid the pitfalls and seek an advisor who knows the ropes.

Watch for outdated information and outdated experience. As an example, I entered this industry in 2009/2010 and was quickly told by many laundromat folks that my pricing should be 10 cents/lb on my washers. Can you believe that there are still people in our industry giving that same outdated advice in 2021? Crazy, absolutely crazy!

Due to so many technology, manufacturing, and customer standards and preferences, this industry, in a matter of a decade, has simply left the old school in the dust, and they may not even know it. They think they know the industry well because they've owned a laundromat or two for a long time, and that's just not how education and knowledge works. It's progressive.

The great thing is that the flipside is true as well. If we want to learn how to do things at an elite level, study the best people with the best *operations*. Notice that I didn't say, study the ones with the nicest or newest stores, or study the ones with the most stores?

I've observed that those with the nicest or newest stores are usually not actually the top operators in our industry. They usually focus on growing their number of stores and/or focus simply on their facilities, and believe that is enough. Nice, state of the art facilities, are NOT enough. If your operations and team are not "top of the industry" then that store won't be state of the art for very long.

These operators say things like, "Build a nice store, keep it clean, and you'll do well." While that may be true for a percentage of operators and stores, my motto for advice like that is that they make favorable rival stores! Favorable for you or me, that is.

Seriously though, if you are in that category and are offended by my words, please know that this book is meant for you too. It is to challenge, teach, and encourage. Please know that I want you to be and do, better. I've written this book to help you do that. You can be offended and prideful, or you can be self-reflective, humble, and willing to grow. The choice, like the many covered so far, is yours.

ELEVATING THE INDUSTRY

Can we have top of the industry operations, AND have the newest or the most laundromats? Sure, absolutely, but my observation is that this is rarely the case. Most laundromat owners simply see their business as selling a commodity and that's it. Even when they build nice stores originally, it's rare that the reinvestment is made in keeping the facilities nice. It's even more rare to have nice, modernized facilities with outstanding operations and customer service.

So here's what I've learned about operations, pivoting, pricing, profits, and yes, value proposition. The operators that are providing the best value proposition are also charging the highest prices in the industry AND, they often-times have the busiest stores with the best team and the best operations. I call these industry leaders trailblazers!

This is not only true of self-serve, but for drop off laundry services, pickup and delivery, vending, gaming, soap sales, etc. These operators are simply amazing. I estimate that these people are roughly the top ten percent of the laundromat industry, along with other industries as well. They are also making the most profits.

There are those that argue this with me, but I've operated at the bottom of the industry, in the middle, and at the top. I've also spent a decade studying those same operations. TRUST ME, the top of the industry is the most profitable. Those at the bottom of the industry just use this as a way of justifying their lack of operations.

Again, this book is here to challenge you to be better, not to shame you. I've been there and you CAN do better for your community, your business, and your family. It's the ideal win/win/win and that is what I want for our industry.

What I often see is an owner trying to juggle operations and acquisitions, and he or she ends up with unfocused growth (or lacking the big picture). Yes, both can be done, but only if you've invested in and built a very strong team. Without a strong team and operations, instead of being all things to all people, you'll end up being nothing to no one.

Team

As I've mentioned and it's worth honing in: A strong team allows you, the owner, to focus on growth and vision, while they focus on operations. These teams are to compare and learn from—or possibly the team you compete with in your market. Unfortunately, too often in a business small or large, the owner doesn't have a strong team of managers and leaders in place. That deficit is often their downfall when they attempt to grow.

Prices

The best laundromat owners are focused on continual improvement of their operations, viable income streams, and improving their value proposition. By default, what ends up happening is their expenses usually go up too and how do they respond? Like any other sophisticated business owner in the world, if our value proposition goes up, then the price goes up too. Nope, not a little and certainly not a silly quarter or two. Their prices go up dramatically, just as their value goes up.

There was a time when I was studying these theories to see if they held water. I want to point out that these are no longer theories or even ideas that I'm throwing out, these are facts. I can confidently say this because of the hundreds, if not thousands of conversations that I've had with operators at all levels of our industry since 2010. They happen in every market in the country, so, no, your market isn't unique or different, ok?

Some are uncomfortable raising their prices or "taking advantage of people" and even tell me that I should be ashamed to make money this way. To you I say, please reach out to me and let's discuss, because this is the most ridiculous thing that I've ever heard.

Let me ask you a question. Who is better serving their community, the people that I bought these stores from or me? The beauty of a free market is that we have plenty of competitors in Cincinnati and if our value proposition versus price were out of whack, then our customers would tell us by using a competitor's business.

Given that our businesses continue to have record growth year over year, I think the community that we serve is speaking loud and clear. Ironically, when an isolated customer leaves for a rival store, we almost always see them, and welcome them back in a few weeks. They almost always realize that they were shopping price only, not value, and that value almost always brings them back to Queen City Laundry.

Now at roughly year five in my laundromat journey, I'd learned that being obsessive about studying, networking with and learning from the best operators in the industry had really elevated my education about business to an elite level. No MBA needed and there was no way that I was stopping!

With a new store in tow, I was about to take all of this knowledge and apply it to take our small business, and awesome team to the next level. And, that we did.

ELITE

I must reiterate the value of seeking the best, the elite, and learning from them. I know many elite operators that own 1 or 2 stores, and they operate business models that we should aspire to. We can learn so much from them. It's absolutely astounding. They are often quietly going about killing it in their local market.

In fact, that's another reason that I've written this book. Rather than keep all this knowledge a secret, I want to shout it from the mountain tops for all to hear. If some in the industry choose to attack me for it, then I'll take that heat.

We continued building our brand Queen City Laundry. With construction and renovations at QCL3 well under way, it was due time to use my research to decided attendant hours and the feasibility of offering a professional drop off laundry service. What I'd learned is that whenever a top operator evolved or pivoted from unattended or partially to fully attended, within 12-18 months their revenue increased enough to cover the additional labor plus some. Yup, you read that correctly. In almost all cases their businesses were better *and* much more profitable.

One quick win was to convert our Milford store (QCL2) into a fully attended store with a drop off laundry service in a fairly short time. Knowing that this was consistent across the industry, I dove in headfirst with this new store and committed to being fully attended. With that investment being made, we simultaneously made the decision to offer a premium drop off laundry service as well.

I spent the next few months obsessed with and studying everything that I could about being an attended laundromat and offering a drop off laundry service. Our goal was and is, to always do everything at an elite level, but we knew that we had a long way to go.

Before I continue from a subheading of Elite, I'll be clear that never have I, or our total Queen City Laundry team, been elitist. By elite, that means we continuously strive to be the best in our work ethic, our quality of service, our standards. These are but some of the standards of a top of the industry model for doing business—any business really.

You should know too, that when a random podcast listener coined me *The Laundromat Millionaire* and we decided on the name of this book, I was reluctant. I may be staunch in knowing what I know and proud of doing what I've done, yet also as a guy from meager means, my core is one of humility. And, a heart of giving back.

So, I had to give that a good think. What it boils down to, however, is that if I can—*you* can.

Laundromat Millionaire are two words not often combined.

If we are going to elevate our industry, we better get used to the term. *Continuing…*

Over the next 6-12 months, we renovated the Anderson store - into becoming our nicest store to date, without question. Over those same 6-12 months our self-service revenues grew in gross sales, we aggressively raised our vend prices, and our drop off laundry sales exploded. After only about a year of operational pivoting, our Anderson store was now our most profitable store by almost 2X.

Not to simplify things too much, but the outcome is one of the beauties of building a team, a brand, training processes, and operations that are top-notch and fully scalable. Once you do this, you can fairly easily take those processes and move them to your other locations, and accelerate your growth across all channels of your business.

We knew that we still had a ton to learn about this new top of the industry model that we were chasing, but we also had learned enough to know that this was the direction we needed to be headed.

To the next level…

OWN THE GRIT WITHIN:

- *Replicate what is working. And, find out where there is another gap you can fill.*

- *Whenever you reach the point where you think you have it all figured out, just remember, there's likely hundreds of people that know more than you. Seek them, embrace a relationship with them, learn from them and always, always, always return the favor with an insane amount of value.*
- *Be a giver not a taker!*

SECTION 4

VENTURE ON. . .

Chapter 14

VENTURE ON!

*"You venture into the unknown land because that is
where your heart will take you. In the end, it is not what
you want to do, it is something you have to do."*
—Laura Ingalls Wilder

*"We grew to our present size almost against ourselves. It was not a
deliberately planned commercial venture in the sense that I sat down
and said that we were going to make ourselves into a huge financial
octopus. We evolved by necessity. We did not sit down and say to
ourselves, 'How can we make a big pile of dough?' It just happened."*
—Walt Disney

While turning our focus back to our Milford Store, I noticed that this store
was busting at the seams for the small, 2100 square foot space that we had.
Now generating a super consistent, self-serve business, and with nowhere
to really grow, I spent some time in the store observing, well, everything.

I was observing our store attendants' performance, as well as the efficiencies and inefficiencies the small space was consistently causing. We had crammed in a lot of washers and dryers, but we couldn't bust through the ceiling we'd hit in revenue. I observed that it wasn't a matter of attracting more customers, but the constraints of our limited space and layout. We had a congestion and workflow problem, or as I eventually termed it, **throughput**.

Having built this store in my first 12 months in business, I'd learned a ton since that time, and I was seeing red flags galore. I noticed things like customers loading washers, then waiting in their cars. Then loading the dryers, and again waiting in their cars. Then, I'd observe them folding at our four folding tables, and often having to move to allow others to get by them.

THE TERM "WONK" IS A COMMON TERM USUALLY REFERRING TO SOMEONE THAT IS EXTREMELY SPECIALIZED, BUT NOT DIVERSE IN THEIR THINKING. IT'S USUALLY USED IN AN ENDEARING WAY. KINDA LIKE A GENIUS.

My findings regarding our throughput, our efficiency, and ease of use even, were terribly alarming. I learned that we had many potential customers coming to our store, and leaving without doing laundry. When I'd catch them leaving, they'd tell me that there wasn't enough room and things were too tight. I learned that our TPD, or turns per day, were quite low for the industry.

I knew the reason was that rather than focus on throughput and customer experience, I'd made the cardinal sin of focusing on cramming as much equipment as possible into this space. I estimate that 90% of the laundromats out there have done the same thing. I challenge you to copy my sit and watch exercise, and if you find you have this situation, it's time to switch it up.

The reason this typically happens is many well-meaning manufacturers, distributors, and even financing companies like to focus on the data only. These organizations are often full of "data wonks," and the data is usually wrong or at least flawed in my opinion. It's even worse that these same organizations have also driven the narrative and flow of information in our industry for many years now. While most of them have good, honest people, the narrative that they often believe and disseminate, is incorrect.

Please keep in mind that I'm not here to suggest that a laundromat could have too few washers and dryers and be successful either. However, it's actually more likely that could happen than if we had too many machines. It's really astounding to me the number of beautiful laundromats being built across the country by well-intentioned people, only to see them filled with 100 washers, 100 dryers and 5-foot aisles with 7 folding tables and 5 seating units.

I'm no rocket scientist folks, but I can do basic addition and subtraction and it just doesn't work. What is a customer to do? Fold their laundry in the car? Just remember that in everything you do in ANY business, the keys to success are value and throughput. These are how we best serve our communities and our families.

You may find that your business can be more profitable, and provide a better customer experience, with fewer machines in your store. I'd even go so far as saying that it's highly likely.

QUICK STORY: CASE IN POINT

Here's how the stereotypical narrative goes for building or renovating a laundromat in most cases:

Laundromat owners must put together a business plan and pro forma for a project in order to get financing approval. They usually don't have experience doing this and/or they just believe this is a good location, so they put together the project with the distributor as their "mentor".

Value and Throughput

Now, we all know that the laundromat industry is full of both good and bad distributors, but even many of the good ones fall into the same trap. The trap is that more equipment equals more revenue, and more revenue equals more profit. You may be shocked to know that this is completely and totally false in most cases.

You may now ask me, "Dave, then how do I generate more revenue and profit for my store?"

I may sound like a broken record, but the answer is VALUE and THROUGHPUT.

Value drives branding, reputation, growth, and customer satisfaction, which then causes people to behave in the way that you want. Meaning, stay put. Do your laundry and please come back.

Once customers are in the store, and see that the store is clean, comfortable, effectively operated, and efficient, they begin to do what they came there to do. Laundry. Can you hear them in your head, silently breathe a sigh of relief, and say to themselves, "I'll get in and out of here quickly, without the hassle of waits or bumping into others in close quarters."

Throughput allows customers to complete their laundry as quickly as possible, gets them home or off to another responsibility, and most often ensures they will return.

You made it easier for that customer. Make it easier for many.

Take it to the bank—a great experience starts and continues with your store producing due to throughput. That's all that matters folks.

CROSS-INDUSTRY BEST PRACTICES

And, this level of thinking is not unique to our industry - whether it is called process re-engineering or my preferred term, throughput.

I have friends that are super successful in the restaurant world, and this is something that most restaurants owners or managers understand and execute very well. Their chefs, cooks and servers likely understand it too, no matter what they may call it. The conscious effort on 'throughput', leads to output…and, service leading to welcome positive feedback, a nice raise or a good tip.

It is a simple argument to make, that the Laundromat Industry can learn many best practices from other industries. Studying other industry verticals in addition to my own, is how I've learned a lot about business. Quickly.

We, as an industry, must get out of this self- contained bubble, check our egos at the door, and move forward into the 21st century. If we do this together, then we will ALL be better for it. When you hear me refer to "elevating our industry", this is a pivotal aspect of what I'm talking about, and it's a win/win for everyone.

Outcomes of Improving Throughput

By now, you probably have guessed what happened next. YUP, I implemented what I learned. I took on a reno (renovation) project in our Milford laundromat. The goal—greater throughput.

Good luck or good timing, the tenant in our neighboring space had vacated, e.g., no more tattoo parlor next door. This gave us the perfect opportunity to remove the wall, expand upon, and redesign our cramped space. This project was actually more like a new build than it was a renovation or "retrofit" as we call this in the laundromat industry, but I dove in.

I'm guessing you're sensing a pattern here in my behavior and risk taking, and you'd be right. The thing that you must remember is that every day, every week, and every month, I was still digging deep into learning and my education was increasing. The more that I learned and the more people that I met, the more that I realized I was doing the absolute right thing for my customers, my community, and for my family.

As the General Contractor, I self-managed this project from beginning to end but did none of the work. Among the permits, contractors, appointments, bids, and other details, it was much more than I bargained for, but after about 6 months, we came out the other side.

Having spent about $110,000 on the project, it was an absolute goldmine for us. Fully attended with a premium Drop Off Laundry Service, we now had two 8-10 foot aisles between our new mega folding tables. In fact, we had a 1 to 1.2 dryer capacity (which is ideal), nice wide aisles on the dryer side of the store, about 5X the folding table capacity that we'd had before, and about 6X the seating space with room to spare. (In the future we plan to widen the washer side of the store to match the ideal layout of our expansion.)

Not adding a single washer, we did exactly as anticipated. We nearly doubled our revenue over the next 8 months. The store was now our biggest, nicest store and setting records every week in self-serve business alone.

Add in our Drop Off Service, vending, and games revenue, and this store rained returns. The irony and beauty of this entire project is that while, it wasn't easy, this store has never had any of our own personal cash invested into it.

According to Robert Kyosaki, mega-bestselling author of *Rich Dad, Poor Dad*, it's an infinite return. Meaning that this asset was built solely by leverage or OPM (Other People's Money). To some, that sounds very dangerous. But remember, it's all based on knowledge and education first. Where people get themselves into trouble with leverage and debt is when they don't start with the knowledge.

Now with three stores in our portfolio that were all highly profitable, a commercial building that was also an infinite return (no cash out of pocket), highly scalable training processes, interviewing processes, a rock star general manager, and a mature, highly skilled team of 16 employees, I knew that we were well on our way.

Family Vacation

We were on our way literally - to our family vacation that summer. I had some apprehension about how all would run in our absence. Every year, our family would take a 1-week vacation out of town, and it usually was the most stressful week of the year for my family, myself, and our GM, Marlene.

This year was different. This year, we left for our 9-day vacation, with our most significant business operations underway to date. Guess what happened???

Nothing… absolutely nothing happened!

We left, never heard from Marlene while we were gone, and when we returned, I realized that everything was still smooth sailing. Having read many times about owning a business, rather than a job, I'd always strived for this situation. My short-term goal was to situate my businesses where I could leave for a week or two, and I'd not be missed. It had finally happened. I find that this is one of my most proud accomplishments in business.

I was so proud, because I realized that I'd built a team of true professionals and systems that were fully scalable. It's not easy, but it really only requires a great work ethic, a lot of knowledge, and a good deal of grit. For the first time in my life, I had significant assets that didn't require me to be around or even available.

Now THIS was true financial freedom! Who am I kidding, that's pure freedom.

OWN THE GRIT WITHIN:

- *We all have potential and, yes, some more than others. Truth is - your potential or ceiling is raised by you, not by some random happenstance in most cases.*
- *Look around, this world needs you to be the best version of yourself. Your community, your family, and your team need you to raise the ceiling on your potential.*
- *Freedom is yours in the making.*

Chapter 15

ROUND THE NEXT CURVE

*"Perfection is not attainable, but if we chase perfection,
we can catch excellence."*
—Vince Lombardi

I've never believed in perfection, but it's something for which I constantly strive. Perhaps that does make me a perfectionist. Most people won't ever even consider striving for perfection because it sounds like, and frankly it is, a lot of work. However, I've learned that if I chase perfection, then I'm already ahead of the curve. With this attitude as my guiding light, I'm not afraid to just keep going.

I gotta go there again with the **Never Give Up** mentality!

Maybe it was time to round yet another curve on this path. About a year after that freedom vacation, we took on our most ambitious project yet. A 5400 square foot laundromat. Again, in a great location. Again, a complete and total dump. Again, poorly run. And, yes again, losing money.

I'd learned so much in the previous 6 years that it came together quickly and smoothly. I went through the process of due diligence, negotiations, layout measurements, equipment decisions, lease negotiations, writing business plans, competitive analysis, arranging financing, etc. etc.

Being my constant, and an understanding wife, and also being a quick-witted bookkeeper, Carla pointed out that every time we bought a new asset it was losing money. Since this *was* always the case with our new asset acquisitions, we were constantly reinvesting our profits from our existing businesses into our newest business. We both realized what was right (we both were) - and, we proceeded to acquire our fourth retail laundromat, QCL4, in Mt. Washington, within the city limits of Cincinnati, Ohio.

With this project, we had all of our ducks in a row before we even closed on the asset or signed a lease. In fact, during lease negotiations, I did my best to acquire this 10,000sq foot strip mall, but was unable to convince the property owner to sell. I did however negotiate the next best thing, which was a right of first refusal for the entire 30 years of the lease term. A right of first refusal simply is a right to match any offer on the property, should it be offered for sale.

In addition to falling in love with the laundromat industry, I'd also fallen in love with purchasing the real estate that my stores were in. While I didn't get to acquire the property at this time, I was assured that at some point the real estate would be mine, if I chose to purchase it.

This planning and diligence allowed us to make rapid fire progress. Along with tremendous progress, once again, came tremendous growth and over the next 12 months came profitability.

In early 2016, we found ourselves with four assets in retail laundromats that were all wildly profitable. I'd hit age 40 and, I reveled in witnessing the potential and opportunities that God had placed in front of me.

I began to see these blessings as actually more like obligations, not in a negative sense, but in a very inspirational and positive sense. These obligations were my way of seeing that there was not a ceiling to my success or in my life. My upbringing mattered as it developed my grit. And, I honor it.

I was just getting started. The sky as the limit to my potential.

All that I could think about was how I didn't want to let my community, my family, my team and my God down. And, I wouldn't.

CLEAN SHOW

Always seeking to be better than the day before, I continued on with my journey and thirst for knowledge and education. That next natural step was to join industry professionals at the Clean Show. The Clean Show is the premier event for the commercial laundering, dry cleaning, and textile service industry. Thousands of people from around the world come to see the newest and most technologically advanced products the industry has to offer.

The Clean Show is a combination textile, dry cleaning, and laundromat trade show held in the U.S every other year. While these industries aren't large enough to each have their own show, they have combined for many years to put on a pretty impressive display. Anyone and anything that is even remotely relevant in our industry is at the CLEAN Show, making it a phenomenal resource for learning and networking.

At this point, I had already attended a few CLEAN Shows but for some reason, I saw this one as different. I suppose it was that for the first time in the industry that I felt like I belonged. As you may imagine, for a guy that's a self-professed laundry nerd, this was my element. Networking with, learning from, and researching everything new in our industry is where I want to be, and there I was.

While spending hours walking the floor, and attending the educational sessions put on by the Coin Laundry Association or other trade-show partners, one thing in this show stood out to me. Software. YUP, I started thinking expansion, throughput, and maybe even additional time leverage—e.g., the future, our future.

I visited a booth for a software company created by a laundromat owner who had launched his own pickup and delivery service, and evidently needed to build a better POS—point of service system—to operate it more effectively.

This was another potential service arm of a service business, to serve a need.

If you recall this time in history, early 2017, it was around the same point that Uber, Door Dash, Grub Hub, and the likes were exploding onto the scene. Our society was having this epiphany about our time and convenience being exceptionally valuable to us, and rapidly moving toward a service driven economy.

Having been someone that is fascinated by human thought patterns, behaviors, and demographics, I'd been studying trends, inventions, gadgets, and basically innovation for years. No, I didn't buy my family

THE CLEAN SHOW IS THE PREMIER EVENT FOR THE COMMERCIAL LAUNDERING, DRYCLEANING, AND TEXTILE SERVICE INDUSTRY. THOUSANDS OF PEOPLE FROM AROUND THE WORLD COME TO SEE THE NEWEST AND MOST TECHNOLOGICALLY ADVANCED PRODUCTS THE INDUSTRY HAS TO OFFER.

members matching Snuggies for Christmas, a set of Ginzu knives or something more practical like a remote car starter. Instead, I went heads down into what could precisely (perfectly) pertain to my businesses.

On day two of the CLEAN Show, I stood in this small, makeshift booth at the back of the conference center and listened to this laundromat turned software guy talk. For over five hours I listened and learned about his software, and how laundry pickup and delivery was our future, and how his software was a leg up for customer service management.

After nearly an entire day of listening, observing, and asking questions of him and his staff at the booth, I left that day with a singular focus on my obsessive brain:

Our Queen City Laundry team and leadership was perfectly positioned to meet a growing demand and need for a laundry pickup and delivery service.

I spent the rest of the show talking shop about our industry, and picking people's brains about wash, dry, fold, and pickup and delivery. I tumbled into loads of new information. While sitting in the airport to board my flight back to Cincinnati, I spoke with my GM, Marlene, on the phone about the show.

I told her, with traditional Dave Menz-ism excitement, that our next venture was into laundry pickup and delivery.

I'll never forget her no-hesitation response. She said, "Dave, you know I'm on board for whatever you want to do, so let's do this!" This reaction is just one of the many qualities that make Marlene such a competent and confident GM (e.g., ROCKSTAR)!

PICKUP AND DELIVERY

Over the next few months, I poured my entire heart and soul into all things pickup and delivery. Amazingly, I found sparse information on this subject. While it had been common for many years in a few bigger markets, the truth was that outside of NYC and Los Angeles, most people had never heard of such a thing. I then realized that if I were going to do this, I was going to have to learn through the school of hard knocks (again).

Never one to shy away from a challenge, I was all in on this new venture for a few reasons. First, I'd already seen the societal shift in mentality toward personal services, and the value that consumers placed on their time. I saw this as a pent up demand for a service like this. The second reason is that I researched the most hated household chores in America, and laundry was #2 on the list, just behind cleaning bathrooms.

Remember, I'm gung ho by now, to elevate the reputation of the laundromat industry and another way to do so was to enhance the laundry experience by filling a gap. So, I factored these things into my equation, looked over my shoulder to the left, to the right, no one there. I asked myself, "Ok, who is best positioned to meet this newfound demand for a laundry service delivered right to your door?"

Low and behold, the answer to my question was me. Well, maybe not me, but us—THE INDUSTRY PROFESSIONALS/OWNERS. Laundromat owners were the answer to the puzzle. We all had an insane amount of excess equipment capacity, in our stores. Even the busy laundromats have this available at strategic times, especially in overnight hours. Make a note of that - especially overnight hours.

The business model geek in me then thought, "All I have to do is figure out the formula or code and the sky is the limit for us." I didn't have the answer and I knew that someone in NYC or LA likely couldn't help a Midwest guy in Cincinnati, Ohio, and I wasn't afraid to take a chance. I also quickly realized that since my team was amazing, and I wasn't needed in my stores anymore, that I had the time to research and learn this business and exact the business model.

Operating with many different, substantial revenue streams that were increasingly healthy, coupled with the fact that we still hadn't increased our personal lifestyle, I was perfectly positioned to cash flow any losses as we cracked the code to this new business.

Let the secret sauce sleuthing begin.
I identified a few other laundry pickup and delivery software companies, in addition to the guys at the CLEAN Show. I talked with, vetted, and received demos from them to make the best possible choice of which to use. They were all ok, but one stood out. The software itself was comparable to others. What really sold them for me was that the owner seemed to have a vested interest in my success. I would be one of their first licensees.

Realizing this would place my business as a focus in their new venture into this market, I saw this as a good thing. I signed the licensing agreement, and off we went into the great unknown. Regardless of my studiousness in attempting to bridge a hefty learning curve, I really had no idea what I was getting into. Who knew the vastness of the learning curve in laundry wilderness?

Over the next 12-18 months we launched and grew our own brand of laundry pickup and delivery in Cincinnati. Using the software to manage, run, and grow our business, we grew with gross revenues exceeding $25,000 per month. I saw this as 'not bad' for our market size, and only having three vans. But, we had a problem. We weren't actually making any money.

Carla and I would talk about it regularly, but I mostly discounted her concerns because we had plenty of money from our other businesses. I was only focused on market share or finding new customers, figuring profits would come with growth of market share. We'd built a substantial delivery business that I was very proud of, and I figured if we grew big enough, we'd eventually start making money by default.

Man, was I wrong.

ROUNDING THE NEXT CURVE WITH PICKUP & DELIVERY

As had been the case for many years, my hard working and super patient wife was sitting at her desk doing her weekly bookkeeping for all of our businesses. It was a Saturday afternoon and she looked more stressed than usual.

She finally let loose. "*David!* You can't keep going like this. I know you're proud of the new delivery business gross revenue, but every month it's getting harder and harder to pay the bills. We're losing money and we can't keep this up forever!"

Stunned at her outburst, I looked at her with wrinkled brow, and said, "How can this be? How can we be losing money when we're making more than ever before?" We argued with each other until we both needed a break.

The next day, she calmly approached me, and we agreed we needed to talk about this 'delivery stuff'. Carla came prepared. She presented me with the fact that we were generating about $25,000 per month in gross revenue, but our delivery business was generating expenses of over $30,000 per month. Moreover, it was getting worse, not better, as we grew. (Have I mentioned that I love my highly educated, data driven, math nerd of a wife, even when she lets me have it?)

I sat there digesting all of this data and information and, if I'm honest, I was devastated. I was so proud of the business that we'd built, but the data didn't lie.

Crack the Code

That very day, I committed to Carla that I'd dig deep, super deep, into the pickup and delivery aspect of our business and I'd fix this. I agreed that after 18 months of tough, hard work we shouldn't be losing thousands of dollars every month. I also owned up to this needing to be fixed, and fixed right now!

Over the next 6 months, I tore apart the pickup and delivery business from the top down looking at every possible loss and inefficiency. What I found was absolutely astonishing, but quite possibly accelerated my knowledge of business in a way that no university or mentor possibly could.

I had to go through it. I couldn't go around it.

I found that while finding profitability in a self-serve and drop off laundry business was relatively easy, finding profitability in the laundry pickup and delivery space was difficult. I combed over data for weeks to find the different places where we were losing money. This was not much fun for someone that isn't necessarily data or numbers driven.

What I learned is that nearly anyone with a laundromat can run pickup and delivery. It's really as simple as hiring drivers to go get and return the laundry, and also as simple as hiring people to physically do the laundry. It is difficult because the logistics side of the business and the processing of laundry side are both very labor intensive, especially if you strive to do them at an elite level.

In knuckling down on our numbers, the logistics side of the business would eventually take care of itself. However, I did find inefficiencies in our routes. There were inefficient zip codes on the outskirts of our service area that, after nearly two years of trying to penetrate that market, just needed to be eliminated.

There were also ways to redesign our routes and pickup/drop off days that would make them more efficient. We dissected these and redesigned them. This helped a lot with our profitability, and we also could see predictable patterns in our logistics that would solve themselves as we continued to gain market share. It was encouraging to know we were at least heading in the right direction.

Next learning point?
Our laundry processors training, management, and work environment were inefficient. We made changes, tested them, and then made more changes again. We looked at our hiring, accountability, and quality control processes, and virtually every one, needed improvement.

We exhausted every possible tool in our tool belt to create efficiencies by purchasing rolling shelves and racks, setting up rolling workstations on the floor, and eventually converting our processing team from second shift over to third shift. Since our self-serve laundry closed at 10pm, we processed a majority of the day's orders when the store was closed to the public. This allowed us to maximize our turns per day.

Additionally, it enabled our laundry processors to work about the store more efficiently by eliminating competition with our self-serve customers for washers, dryers, folding tables, laundry carts, etc. (Remember: The aforementioned secret sauce of overnight hours?) With every one of these improvements, we tested everything, then we tweaked the processes and retested again.

Lastly and importantly, we changed our standard hourly pay compensation structure for our laundry processors. Our goal was to create natural incentives in both their job performance and compensation, in order to incentivize them to produce at a much higher rate of speed, while also avoiding any sacrifice in the quality of the finished product.

Incentivize Your Well-Deserving Team
This entire change process may not sound grueling or impressive, but imagine you're an employee or even business owner and nearly every week something is changed or needs to change. As the owner, you must deliver this message to your team knowing that it won't be a fun message, yet must be done.

Open and honest communication is something I truly cannot say enough about. It's the right thing to do, in a real way. It's instrumental in earning and maintaining the trust of your employees, which rolls into the trust with your customers and within your community.

For example, we changed the entire compensation structure for our laundry processors six times over a 9-month period of time. At one point, I literally looked my entire team in the eyes and simply told them the following:

"Guys look, I'm not even going to pretend that I know what I'm doing because I don't. I am committing to you guys that I will figure this out and when I do, we will all have a great job with a healthy and profitable company. We will grow and scale this business to new heights, and I will commit to you that I will be sure that the company's profitability never comes at the expense of our employees.

I am committed to finding a happy medium, but in the meantime, I need you to hang in there with me. Give me your ideas and feedback, and we'll figure this out together. If you're not up for this ride and want to leave, I completely understand, but the truth is, I don't have a choice. If I don't keep making changes until we figure this thing out, then my only option is to shut this business down, and you won't have a job."

Lucky for me, I didn't lose any of our best team members during this chaos. They all stuck around and have been duly rewarded. Our pickup and delivery business began to flourish in ways that I'd never imagined and, yes, we eventually saw a profit that I knew would increase as we scaled the business.

Cracking the code on pickup and delivery was an incredibly grueling process from beginning to end and a lot of sweat and tears. I estimate that it took the majority of a year. Slowly but surely, with continuous improvements and communication along the way, we made and managed change—until we found our sweet spot. This was the spot where the company was fully scalable from an operations standpoint, and where we could also afford to pay and reward our rockstar employees for their hard, and exemplary, work.

We'd done it! Our team cracked the code!

Exhausted? Maybe. Proud? Beyond measure.

OWN THE GRIT WITHIN:

- *Too many people focus on gross numbers. Things like number of stores, turns per day and even pounds of laundry processed. But, there are only two things that matter in business, - happy employees and customers, and healthy profits.*
- *While "cracking the code" may sound like a cool catchphrase, it's actually a pretty grueling process. Too many times, small business is glamorized as a fun and lucrative endeavor. Truth is that the stress that I put my team, family and myself through was very tough.*
- *Is cracking the code worth it? Yell to the hills and back—YES!*

Chapter 16

CHANGING COMMUNITIES AND CHANGING LIVES

"I alone cannot change the world, but I can cast a stone across the waters to create many ripples."
—Mother Teresa

In the end, after almost three years of grinding in all, with the efforts and patience of our entire team, we'd, indeed, cracked the code on pickup and delivery laundry, and found the sweet spot. That reward of "cracking the code" increased the profitability of that one laundromat we run our pickup and delivery business out of, by 3X (times).

I was more relieved than possibly ever in life.

Maybe it took me a minute (figuratively) to realize the *Code*, was much bigger, much more substantial. Part of being a small business owner is the constant stress in knowing that you are directly responsible for your team's livelihood and well-being. If you mess up the business and it goes under, yes, you are ruined. But, your employees lose their jobs too. I've always taken this responsibility very seriously.

When employees lose jobs or businesses close, there is a ripple effect. The chaos it can create in families who have bills to pay and food to put on tables—well, it is something I personally never want to experience again. Most definitely, I do not want it for the quality people I have the blessed fortune to work with every day.

And, I also consider the economic effects of supply, and creating demand, as well as beautifying a neighborhood. While I'm proud of all of our business accomplishments, I'm probably most proud of the fact that we stuck it out, and did the hard work necessary.

THE LAUNDROMAT MILLIONAIRE

Shortly after figuring out the model with Pickup & Delivery, we applied for a business consolidation loan for our company. As part of completing the application process, we were required to update our Personal Financial Statement (PFS). I'd just completed it.

Only surpassed by my marriage to Carla and the births of my children, this was one glorious moment. I sat across the room, taking a deep breath, and felt eyes on me. I looked up and said a phrase I never thought I'd say to my Carla, "Do you realize that we are millionaires?"

Feeling very proud, I just sat there for a few minutes realizing that I'd taken my family from a net worth of roughly 50-60K at age 32, to a net worth of over one million dollars in a matter of only 8 years. I realized that I'd accomplished all of this by starting with only a few thousand dollars in our savings account, and virtually no formal education other than public high school. We'd worked hard at our jobs, saved up about $25,000-$30,000 in seed money, then leveraged that, and took on tremendous risk. We had put in a ton of sweat equity and debt to elevate our family to a net worth of over a million dollars.

If I'm honest though, my pride for this rather arbitrary number of one million wasn't really important to me or Carla at all. And, it still isn't as we arrive at multi-millionaire status. To keep it real though, I'd tell ya that being called The Laundromat Millionaire—a phrase I did not coin—well, it does feel good.

While the money is nice, we take much more pride in the fact that our team of nearly 40 employees now had jobs, good jobs, and that they really enjoyed coming to work every day. We were also proud that we'd changed the local communities in and around Amelia, Anderson, Milford and Mt Washington, Ohio by investing heavily in something as vital to the community as a modernized laundromat.

We now realized something that we hadn't always given as much credence as is deserved. We realized that a local laundromat is an essential and vital community resource. It's not a luxury, but it is a necessity. A local laundromat serves a community in a way that very few outside, and even some in the industry, truly understand.

We are very proud that all four locations had been converted from complete eyesores and community liabilities, into valuable community assets. We had created facilities where people could come to do their laundry in a clean, safe, friendly, and modernized manner.

GRATITUDE

That day, I had another epiphany, a realization if you will. While I'd always loved my little laundromat businesses because they were mine, I now realized something greater. I realized that the laundromat business was the best small business in America, if not the entire world.

I had this tremendous feeling of gratitude come over me for the laundromat industry and for all of the people in it, definitely the good and even the bad. I had gratitude for the bad apples and the dark side of the industry for showing me what not to be and what to avoid. I also had tremendous gratitude for the superstars, my personal caped crusaders. Many of them had showed me, taught me, and inspired me to not be good or even great - but to chase perfection.

I additionally felt gratitude for all those adults, teachers, and not so nice kids that had given me this giant chip on my shoulder by constantly telling me what they believed that I could and couldn't do.

In my acknowledgements forthcoming, I may have to shout out to my bicycle that pumped me up to find bottles, collect 10 cents, and then buy some Now and Later candy to sell for a quarter to some of those said naysayers. Enter the businessman, now…and later… the Laundromat Millionaire.

In any case, as I sat there that day thinking about all we had achieved so far, I had this overwhelming feeling overtake me. It was a tremendous feeling of accomplishment, but even more so, it was a feeling of responsibility and of obligation to those around me. I felt this obligation to continue to strive to be better tomorrow than I was yesterday. I now felt an obligation to elevate my family, those around me, both in and out of the laundromat industry, and to change my family tree for generations to come.

These are the reasons for telling my story, my podcast and for coaching hundreds of fellow entrepreneurs each year.

And, yes, for writing this book.

My hope is that my story helps you better understand what business owners and their families' go through and what makes them who they are or choose to be, but also how vitally important this work is to our communities and world.

Ultimately, my hope is that for the rest of my life, my gratitude and gratefulness come through in everything that I do.

Never give up. Realize the need for grit—and the value it espouses. Keep on keepin' on with learning all you can. Lift your head to say thanks to our God.

Until we meet again…heck, I've gotta get heads down on my mission of elevating our industry—mine being the laundromat industry. If there is proof in this story…there is plenty of proof in elevating an industry—any industry. I just happen to love this one.

Own the grit within. Never give up,

Dave
P.S. Go forth and prosper.

CONCLUSION

I've used a lot of adjectives about myself in this book, like obsessive, stubborn, resolute, bold, passionate, and the one I'll end with here, is **grateful.**

The noun that I'll abide by is **Grit.**

Here I am a couple scoopfuls of years into business ownership, and I am reasonably well known in my industry—maybe more so than I realize. And, that grows every day. I'm pleased with my mission to elevate the laundromat industry, with the pure intention of also impacting lives and helping people realize what is possible.

In the next curve of this journey, I hope I'll be known not only as the Laundromat Millionaire, but as a working man who did good, by being good—to others, his family, his neighbors and our communities. This is a message to anyone aspiring to work in any industry, and move to the elite level—not elitist—but elite, the top model of the best way to do business, and the smart way. I'm finding that sharing my way of doing business and my work ethic, actually raises the value proposition for other industries. Yet, let's leave that for the next book, as I venture on.

Thank you for reading my foray into authorship. Stay in touch with me at www.laundromatmillionaire.com.

To the next level,

Dave

ACKNOWLEDGMENTS

For my God, often I feel so completely inadequate of your love and grace, yet I receive both anyway. I thank you for the adversity, pain and suffering that have molded me into exactly who this world needs me to be. Until I leave this earth, I will strive to honor your sacrifice by serving others and appreciating every opportunity that you place in front of me.

For my Carla, you are simply amazing, and I'm honored that God allowed us to cross paths, raise a family and live our lives together. I'll never read Proverbs 31:10 without thinking how lucky I am to have a supportive, loving and selfless wife as you. I Love You. (Proverbs 31:10 An excellent wife who can find? She is far more precious than jewels.)

For my Tannah, being blessed with you as my baby girl is one of my most grateful blessings. You first made me a Daddy and I wouldn't have it any other way. Your heart and love for every person and animal is unique and one of the many things that I love about you. Never stop being exactly who God made you to be, and always strive to be a better version of that person tomorrow! Daddy Loves You Tt.

For my Madden, having my little entrepreneur who just brings laughter into any room will always make me smile in a way that few others can. Remember that you can accomplish anything that you choose to if you want it bad enough. Never stop being exactly who God made you to be but always strive to be a better version of that person tomorrow! Daddy Loves You Maddog.

For my Rayden, I never dreamed that the baby in our family would be so absolutely amazing. You are unique in every way, including in your compassion and caring for others but also in your wicked intelligence. You have a love and gift for science and building like very few, and I cannot wait to see where that takes you. Never stop being exactly who God made you to be, and always strive to be a better version of that person tomorrow! Daddy Loves You Peanut.

For my grandparents, aunts, uncles, and cousins, thank you for being a part of my life and for helping to mold me into the man that I am today. Some of my fondest memories are with you, and for that I am eternally grateful. I love you all.

For my Mom and Dad, thank you for the countless sacrifices that you've made and for the lessons that you've taught me. I am grateful to have such loving, sacrificial and supportive parents.

For Steve Millman and Marlene Adams, thank you for believing in me and seeing my dreams and vision, and for working tirelessly to help me achieve them. You both believed in me when most did not. You are an amazing people, friends and I'm honored to know you both.

For my team in all of my businesses, my hope is that you know and understand how grateful I am to have each one of you in my organization. Serving others in our communities is something that we do together, and I couldn't do it without you.

For Kristin Andress, thank you for coming into my life at the perfect time and for sharing your gift, heart, and talents with me in this project. You have perfected the ability to lift my rough manuscript into this beautiful book that so perfectly articulates my story, feelings and beliefs. This book would simply not be the finished product that it is, without you.

For all of my Entrepreneurial friends in the world, thank you for being my tribe. Thank you for listening to my hours of rambling, and for being a place where I am understood and appreciated for being exactly who I am. My prayer is that everyone will someday find their tribe, like I have you.

For all of those adults, teachers and peers that thought and told me that I'd never amount to anything...... How do you like me now? Lol

ABOUT THE AUTHOR

Dave Menz is a working class guy from Flint, Michigan who had a determined vision of becoming a business owner. That vision came true as he is now the curator of The Queen City Laundry chain in Ohio, and is known as the Laundromat Millionaire.

Dave grew up in poverty and overcame superhero-like obstacles. His story, revealed in his debut book, *Laundromat Millionaire—The Grit to Elevate an Industry* is a life and business journey that doesn't stop at rags to riches. It *begins* with a stubborn and obsessive mission to be a business owner with a tenacious and genuine purpose to help others to do the same—even if you *also* do not have a college degree or perhaps *because* you have one.

Dave teaches the principles of relentless studying of the greats to be a great, and knowing that even if an industry—like laundry—isn't sexy, you can make it so. His initial foray into business ownership was a side hustle alongside his corporate gig with Cincinnati Bell. He found his first business on Craigslist. (YUP, I did, as Dave would say.) Once he owned it, he overhauled it from struggling, losing money and outdated, to one that was a valuable proposition to serve as a vital community asset. In essence, he cared—for those who needed this service and deserve it.

His vision expands beyond only owning multiple businesses under the auspices of Queen City Laundry. He shares his wisdom on his podcast and is a sought after guest and coach. Always the student, he expands his business model—and reach—to serve needs discovered.

As a picked on kid who was told he had limited options, to his readers, employees, fans and his children, Dave says, "If I can, you can. It simply takes grit." It is with this fortitude, he forges forward in elevating an industry, and likely not only one. Certainly, more lives will be elevated as a result of his Menz-ism touch.

Dave and his family live in Cincinnati, Ohio. He is a family man and a man of faith.

CONNECT WITH DAVE

Facebook- https://www.facebook.com/laundromatmillionaire/
Linkedin- https://www.linkedin.com/in/dave-laundromat-millionaire-menz/
YouTube- https://www.youtube.com/c/LaundromatMillionaire
Instagram- https://www.instagram.com/laundromatmillionaire/

AS SEEN ON OR IN

BUSINESS INSIDER

A free ebook edition is available with the purchase of this book.

To claim your free ebook edition:

1. Visit MorganJamesBOGO.com
2. Sign your name CLEARLY in the space
3. Complete the form and submit a photo of the entire copyright page
4. You or your friend can download the ebook to your preferred device

A **FREE** ebook edition is available for you or a friend with the purchase of this print book.

CLEARLY SIGN YOUR NAME ABOVE

Instructions to claim your free ebook edition:
1. Visit MorganJamesBOGO.com
2. Sign your name CLEARLY in the space above
3. Complete the form and submit a photo of this entire page
4. You or your friend can download the ebook to your preferred device

Print & Digital Together Forever.

Snap a photo

Free ebook

Read anywhere

Printed in the USA
CPSIA information can be obtained
at www.ICGtesting.com
JSHW022344140824
68134JS00019B/1677